£ 14.99

Microsof   r 2:
Do Ama

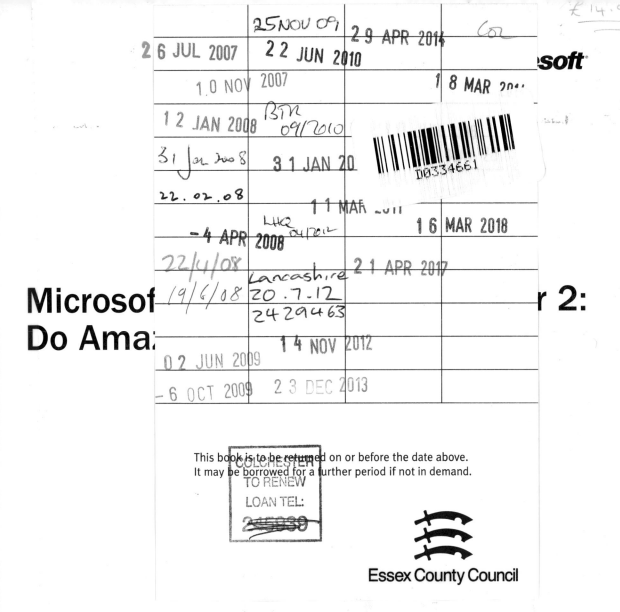

John Buechler

PUBLISHED BY
Microsoft Press
A Division of Microsoft Corporation
One Microsoft Way
Redmond, Washington 98052-6399

Library of Congress Cataloging-in-Publication Data
Buechler, John, 1940-
    Microsoft Windows Movie Maker 2: Do Amazing Things / John Buechler.
       p. cm.
    Includes index.
    ISBN 0-7356-2014-8
    1. Motion pictures--Editing--Data processing.   2. Microsoft Windows Movie Maker.   I.
  Title.

    TR899.B75   2003
    778.5'35'02855369--dc22   2003061590

Printed and bound in the United States of America.

1 2 3 4 5 6 7 8 9   QWT   8 7 6 5 4 3

Distributed in Canada by H.B. Fenn and Company Ltd.

A CIP catalogue record for this book is available from the British Library.

Microsoft Press books are available through booksellers and distributors worldwide. For further information about international editions, contact your local Microsoft Corporation office or contact Microsoft Press International directly at fax (425) 936-7329. Visit our Web site at www.microsoft.com/mspress. Send comments to *mspinput@microsoft.com*.

Microsoft, Microsoft Press, Outlook, Picture It!, PowerPoint, Windows, and Windows Media are either registered trademarks or trademarks of Microsoft Corporation in the United States and/or other countries. Other product and company names mentioned herein may be the trademarks of their respective owners.

The example companies, organizations, products, domain names, e-mail addresses, logos, people, places, and events depicted herein are fictitious. No association with any real company, organization, product, domain name, e-mail address, logo, person, place, or event is intended or should be inferred.

Acquisitions Editor: Alex Blanton
Development Editor: Sandra Haynes
Project Editors: Sandra Haynes and Jean Trenary
Production Editor: Laurie Stewart
Designer/Compositor: Maureen Forys

Body Part No. X10-08421

To Bernadette, who constantly inspires me
to grow and do what is meaningful in life.
—J.B.

To my beautiful bride, Victoria.
Thank you so much for believing in me!
—M.S.T.

CONTENTS

Acknowledgments

Thank you Alex Blanton, acquisitions editor, for believing in this project and constantly being there to gently and firmly pull the needed parts together; Matt Calder and the Movie Maker Team at Microsoft for teaching me the ins and outs of Movie Maker 2; Mike Toot, contributing author, who turned my often dry technical writing style into words that I and others enjoy reading; Sandra Haynes, development and project editor, who wrapped it all into a great package; Jean Trenary, in late and out early but taking the project a big step forward while here; Kim Wimpsett, copy editor, for very thorough and professional reviewing; Laurie Stewart and Maureen Forys, production editor and designer/compositor, respectively, for adding the finishing touches.

—John "PapaJohn" Buechler

Big thank yous go to everyone who helped on this project: Alex Blanton, acquisitions editor, for putting the team together; Sandra Haynes, development and project editor, who kept me on track despite my best efforts to do otherwise; Jean Trenary, who also project edited before taking off for greener pastures (good luck on your new job!); Kim Wimpsett, copy editor, who changed my writing from tolerable to smooth and readable; Laurie Stewart and Maureen Forys, for putting all the pieces together into such a beautiful book; Sachi Guzman, for proofreading the pages; Robert Shackelford, for all the help on the finer points of directing "big budget" movies; and of course to John "PapaJohn" Buechler for being such a knowledgeable resource and all-around great guy to work with.

—Michael S. Toot

Introduction

Welcome to the exciting world of Microsoft Windows Movie Maker 2! Movie Maker 2 is an easy-to-use, friendly, and powerful program you can use to create your own movies, videos, and other amazing shows right on your own home computer. Movie Maker isn't just for home movies. Using Movie Maker, you can work with digital movies, analog video recordings from VCRs, digital photographs, scanned images, songs, sound tracks, sound effects, and just about any visual or audio media you can imagine. If you can get it onto your computer, you can work with it in Movie Maker. Express your creativity, and share home movies with others today!

You don't need a lengthy history of filmmaking or boring discussions about computer software.

Coming Attractions

This book takes you through the process of building a movie from start to finish using only your computer, Movie Maker 2, and any digital media you have available. Your first movie will look, sound, and play like a professional movie; and because you made it, you'll feel the pride of creating something cool and amazing for your friends and family to see.

Once you've made your first movie, you'll learn how to build upon your new movie-making abilities to create other projects using the same steps and tools you've already used. The book is project-oriented, not technology-oriented, so you'll learn what you need to know to get the job done and create amazing projects. There will be no deadlines to meet, tests to take, or deadlines handed out. This book is all about playing and having fun and at the same time discovering just how cool it is to make your own movies in just a few minutes on your own computer.

For those of you who feel the creative fire start to burn and want to learn more, there are projects and topics in Part II of the book that go into more detail than in earlier chapters. These are for the people who work with Movie Maker 2 for a while and then say, "This is cool! What else can it do?" You can read these chapters in any order, and of course, you're encouraged to explore and play with the Movie Maker 2 features on your own.

Who this Book Is For

This book is for people who want to make great movies and create cool effects on a computer. You want to learn how to create movies quickly and simply; you don't need a lengthy history of filmmaking or boring discussions about computer software. You want to jump right in, do it right the first time, and create a cool movie you can show to your family and friends.

You might have bought a computer with Windows Movie Maker 2 on it, or you might have bought a digital camera and capture card and are wondering what to do with them. This book answers your questions and helps you create a fun movie in the very first chapter. From there you can explore the features that Movie Maker 2 has to offer, including professional-quality editing tools, transitions, and publishing capabilities. With just a few clicks and drags, you can produce movies that rival those of any professional video house, without film school or computer science degrees.

How to Use this Book

Start with Chapter 1 and walk through the steps to create your first movie. You can read the chapter first before you start or you can just jump right in; along the way you'll see how to make movies and get just the information you need, when you need it. You can then move on to Chapters 2 through 5, learning how to enhance your movie or create other exciting projects. You can skip around these chapters in any order. You can also read Chapters 6 through 8 in any order, though the topics and projects are a step up from those that preceded them. Do the ones you're comfortable with, and come back to the others when you're ready.

Where You Can Learn More

You can find Movie Maker 2 resources primarily on the Internet. The two key places are Microsoft itself and this book's companion Web site. Microsoft is your first stop for product updates, demo files or free downloads, bug fixes, and general news and information about Movie Maker 2. You can start your quest for information at the Movie Maker home page at *http://www.microsoft.com/windowsxp/moviemaker/*.

If you want more specific help with Movie Maker 2 or this book, you can visit the companion Web site at *http://www.papajohn.org*. The Web site is an online community resource for Movie Maker 2 beginners and professionals alike. The Web site rolls up the information from newsgroup postings, adds what's learned from Microsoft, and annotates the information with real experiences. It's constantly evolving, driven mostly by the collective needs of Movie Maker 2 users. It's a great first place to find additional information about Movie Maker 2, answers to hardware and software questions, and information and projects created by others. In addition, all the project files in this book are on the Web site, so you can download the files and work with them in each chapter. This site is your best resource for information and tips while working with Movie Maker 2.

A Word or Two About Copyrights

Throughout this book you'll be working with digital media that you acquire from different sources. Many of the sources will be your own: your home movies, your pictures or slides, or your shouts of "Surprise!" from the last birthday party you attended. Other sources might be ones you find on the Internet, such as pictures or fonts, or ones from your own music collection or DVDs.

When working with any image or source, whether you created it or someone else did, you're working with copyrighted material. "Copyright" means that the person who created it owns the right to say how that material is used. Just as you have the right to say how your home movies are used, others have the right to say how they want their digital sources used, too. When you use material from other sources, copyright law says that you must ask permission or pay a royalty or licensing fee before you incorporate the material into your projects.

However, you can generally use material from other sources if it's for your personal or private use and won't be distributed or shared with others. This is known as "fair use," and it allows you to create your projects using copyrighted material from other sources. But if you plan to put your projects onto the Internet for the world to see, then you should be aware that you might run afoul of others who believe you've violated their ownership rights in their material. If you can, use source materials that are clearly labeled "free" or "public domain." That way, you might avoid any potential problems with copyright violation. If you want to use materials that aren't labeled as "free" for your use, then be aware of how you distribute or share your final product.

There are many information sources on the Internet about copyrights, digital media, and fair use. If you want to know more, you can start by searching at *http://www.papajohn.org*, or you can do your own Internet research. Have fun, and enjoy making your movies!

PART I

Say goodbye to your raw, unedited footage and hello to compelling, high-quality movies! With your video camera, your computer, and a little bit of time, you can put together movies that you'll be proud to show your friends and family. You'll learn about Microsoft Windows Movie Maker 2 and how to use its tools to assemble video, still images, and audio into movies. Whatever you want to create, Movie Maker 2 will move your creations from being good to simply amazing!

Making Movies with Movie Maker 2

- Take a Tour of Movie Maker
- Organize Your Video Footage
- Capture Video from Your Camcorder
- Create Introductions
- Organize and Edit Your Clips
- Save and Play Back Your Movie

Create Your First Amazing Movie

CHAPTER 1

You don't need a professional editing studio or a degree in computer science to make your own movies. If you can drag, drop, and click, you can quickly create professional-looking movies without having to master complex editing equipment or obscure software packages. Remember, if you've got Microsoft Windows XP, you already have Microsoft Windows Movie Maker 2 on your computer. Movie Maker does more than assemble simple movies from basic clips. It contains sophisticated editing tools and features that let you create new and exciting multimedia presentations that you can run on your computer, on your CD or DVD player, or over the Internet. Are you ready to make a movie? Let's go!

Making a movie is easy when the tools are laid out right in front of you.

Coming Attractions

This chapter shows you how to create your first movie using Movie Maker 2. You'll go through the process, step by step, starting with a quick tour of Movie Maker and then moving right into making your own movie. You'll learn the eight basic steps to follow when making a movie. By the end of the chapter, you'll have a two-minute movie, complete with introduction and closing titles, that you can show to others. But first, let's go through some of the basics.

Getting to Know Movie Maker 2

If Movie Maker 2 isn't installed on your computer, you can download it for free from Microsoft. See the Appendix for more information. If Movie Maker is already installed on your computer, start it up now so you can begin your first project.

To start Movie Maker 2, follow these steps:

1. Click the Start button.

2. Click All Programs.

3. Click Windows Movie Maker.

Figure 1-1 shows the main Movie Maker 2 window. The main window contains all the tools you need to create a movie in one place. The main window is streamlined so you aren't overwhelmed with buttons, tools, or gadgets; all the features you need to use are cleanly and simply integrated into the main window. You'll find that making a movie is easy when the tools are laid out right in front of you.

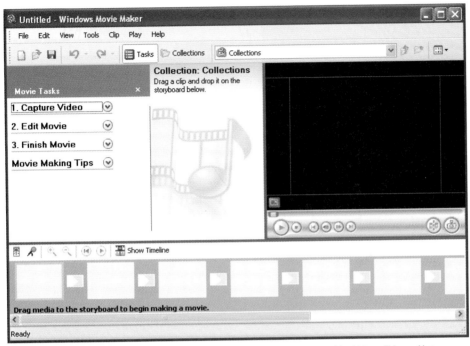

Figure 1-1 The Movie Maker 2 window, showing the menu bar, toolbar, and panes with which you'll be working

NOTE

Depending on how Movie Maker was installed, you might need to click Start | All Programs | Accessories | Entertainment | Windows Movie Maker.

Before you jump in and start creating your first masterpiece, take a moment for a quick tour of the main window. This is where you'll be creating your movie. The tour won't take long, and you'll get a good idea of how each part of the window works to help you create your first movie.

USING THE MENU BAR AND TOOLBAR

The menu bar and toolbar in Movie Maker 2, shown in Figure 1-2, are similar to the ones in other Windows applications you might have used, such as Microsoft Word or Microsoft Outlook. You use the File menu to import source files, save and reopen project files, and save finished movie files. The Edit menu provides common editing commands such as Copy and Paste. The View, Tools, and Clip menus provide commands that are specific to Movie Maker; you'll use several of these commands while you work through the example in this chapter. The Play choices provide similar controls to those under the monitor, which you use to preview clips in collections or the project in the timeline. The Help menu, in addition to providing you with access to online help resources, also provides a command that takes you to the Movie Maker site on the Internet where you can find current information about Movie Maker.

Some commands have alternate ways of activating them, such as by using the context-sensitive menus, by using hotkeys, or by using buttons on the toolbar. It's much quicker to click a toolbar button or press a keystroke combination than to work through menus and dialog boxes; furthermore, they're extremely helpful if you have a repeated task you want to perform. Throughout the book, you'll see these methods described in tasks because they're easy to use and will save you a lot of time. You can usually find the same command by using the menu bar and dialog boxes.

The toolbar has buttons and icons that activate common commands. Some of them will be familiar to you if you've used other Microsoft products, such as the Save Project button that saves all the work you've done in a project. You'll learn about all these toolbar buttons at some point in the book. If you need to know what a button does, hover your mouse over the button for a few seconds, and a ToolTip appears, describing what the button does and any hotkey shortcut that's available.

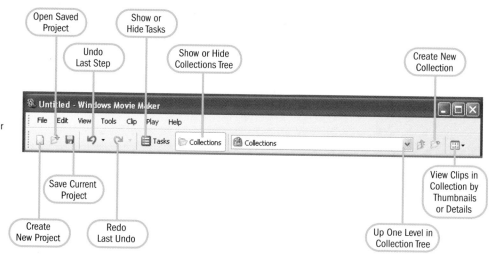

Figure 1-2
You'll use the menu bar and toolbar frequently throughout the movie-making process.

While on the subject of saving files, you should save your project frequently while you work on it. That way you can ensure your creative efforts will always be ready when you come back for "just a few more edits." To save your project, follow these steps:

① Click File | Save Project As.

② You can browse to a different folder or save in the default My Videos folder. It's usually a good idea to create a separate folder for each project so you can keep track of the necessary files in one place.

③ Type a name for your project. Movie Maker automatically adds the file extension .MSWMM to your project.

④ Click Save.

Your project file is now saved. You can also save your file by clicking the Save icon in the toolbar. If you haven't named your project, the Save As dialog box will appear, and you can name your project as usual.

USING THE MOVIE TASKS, COLLECTIONS, AND MONITOR PANES

The middle part of the Movie Maker 2 window is where you'll work with source material and review it in preparation for using the clips in your movies. This is where you get to organize your material and think about how it best fits into your movie. The area consists of three panes: the Movie Tasks pane, which lists tasks for you to complete; the Collections pane, which displays your movie clips, images, sounds, transitions, and video effects; and the Monitor pane, which plays back your clips and movie projects like a VCR.

In the Movie Tasks pane, shown in Figure 1-3, you can see a partial list of tasks to check off while you put your movie together. You can show or hide a list of tasks for each step by clicking the up or down arrows to the right of each step. This chapter follows the task list, but you won't need a few tasks for your first project.

Figure 1-3
The Movie Tasks pane gives you an easy-to-follow task list for making a movie.

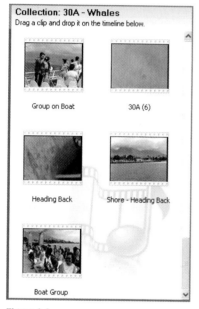

Collection: 30A - Whales
Drag a clip and drop it on the timeline below.

Group on Boat   30A (6)

Heading Back   Shore - Heading Back

Boat Group

Figure 1-4
The Collections pane displays the collection you're currently viewing.

The Movie Tasks pane performs a second purpose: when you click the Tasks and Collections buttons in the toolbar, you switch between the task list and your personal list of source files, such as video clips, music files, still images, audio clips, video transitions, and video effects. The Movie Tasks name changes to Collections, and it displays your list of collections where links to your source files are organized. It works just like Windows Explorer; when you click a collection in the left pane, the clips in it display in the middle Collections pane. Speaking of which....

Unlike Windows Explorer, which has a one-to-one correlation between an icon or item in its list and a file on the hard disk, Movie Maker can have a single clip in a collection that relates directly to a single two-hour video file—or you can divide up the clip in the collection such that you have 200 clips that all relate to the same source file. Splitting clips in Movie Maker doesn't change the file on the hard disk. Some people think that Movie Maker copies the source files; it's more like Power Point in that it just links to them.

Figure 1-4 displays the Collections pane, the middle area in the Movie Maker 2 window that shows you which clips are in the collection selected in the left pane. When you start Movie Maker, it remembers the view you were in the last time you used the software and starts in that view automatically.

TIP

When you get some practice using Movie Maker to create your movies, you probably won't need the task list open all the time or you'll have to switch between the Movie Tasks and Collections views. With experience, most people find it easier to keep the Collections pane visible while working with source files and refer to the Movie Tasks pane only when needed for reminders or instructions. For now, you should keep the Movie Tasks pane visible.

The Monitor pane, shown in Figure 1-5, previews video, previews images and music/audio/video clips in a collection, or previews the project storyboard or timeline while it develops. You can preview any clip by selecting it in the Collections pane and clicking the Play button at the bottom left of the Monitor pane, or you can double-click a clip to play it in the Monitor pane. The Monitor pane also offers you real-time previews of your project. You can mix video, add special effects and transitions, include music and text effects, and then press the Play button to get real-time previewing without waiting for rendering.

The video capture wizard has its own monitor to see the video when it's coming in. It looks like this one, but it's part of a different window. The monitor controls also work for music/audio clips in a collection.

Figure 1-5 The Monitor pane offers playback controls that are used to view and step through your clips and movies in progress.

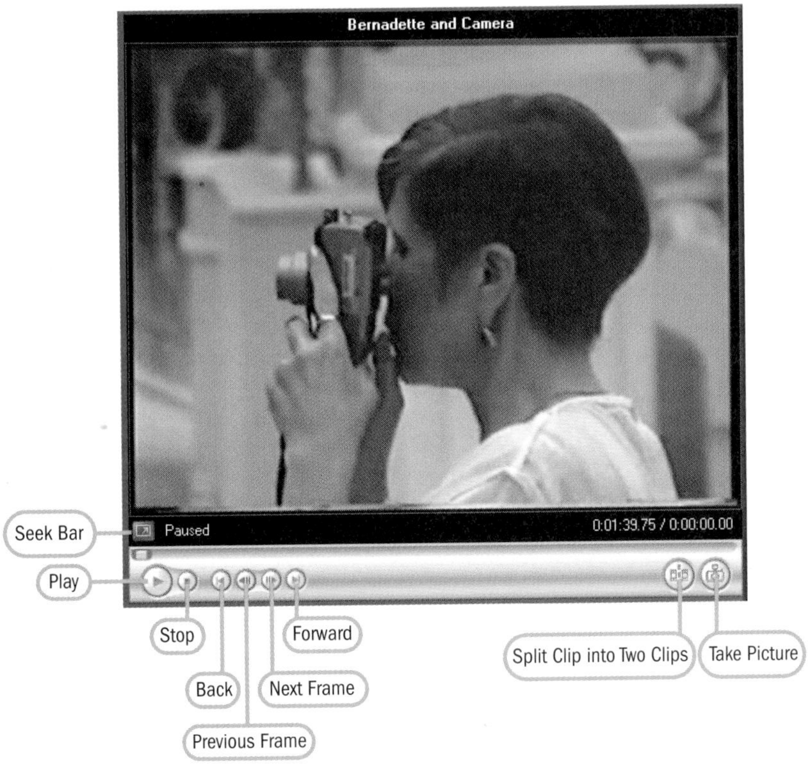

USING THE STORYBOARD AND TIMELINE

The bottom pane is the storyboard or timeline, depending on which view you select. Figure 1-6 displays the Storyboard view. You can toggle between two views by clicking the Show Timeline or Show Storyboard button.

Figure 1-6 The storyboard is where most of the action takes place, including inserting clips and building transitions and effects.

It's here, in the Storyboard or Timeline pane, that you'll assemble and compose your movies. Some people prefer the Storyboard pane, and others prefer the Timeline pane. In later chapters you'll see that each has its advantages, depending on what you're trying to do and the degree of control you need over the project.

Both the storyboard and the timeline allow you to put your movie together using nonlinear editing. One of the great advantages of nonlinear editing is that you can whip up a rough draft of a movie project even quicker than you can write about it. The editing environment is simple yet powerful; you can toggle between the timeline and storyboard as needed. You have lots of options to use, which you'll learn about when you get into intermediate and advanced subject material. You're free to mix anything you want into a movie on the spur of the moment, playing around as much as you want.

You also have the freedom to make changes or back them out, so your experiments are never permanent or painful to fix. In fact, nothing is permanently fixed until you save your project to a CD or DVD. It's like interactive thinking while you draft. And a rough draft can quickly turn into a great—or amazing—movie. So play around without fear of doing something wrong. You can't do anything wrong using Movie Maker.

So now, sit down with this book and Movie Maker, and get ready to make your first movie.

> While you go through the steps to make your first movie, you'll see task items, menu commands, and tabbed dialog boxes that aren't immediately discussed in this chapter. Most of them will be covered in later chapters in other projects. If you have a burning curiosity to explore them now, feel free to go off and investigate. Come back to this chapter when you're ready to make your first movie and pick up where you left off.
>
> **NOTE**

Creating Your Movie

For your first project, you'll create a two-minute movie. A two-minute movie might not sound long, but it's just about the right length for walking through the process of creating a movie using the basic tools in Movie Maker 2. When you've completed this, you'll be familiar with the way that movies are put together, and you'll have a fun first project that you can show to your family and friends. Just remember that this first project doesn't have to be perfect or have a plot that Hollywood would kill to produce. It's your opportunity to have fun, to add silly elements if you want, and to enjoy the ease with which you can create a cool movie on your own computer.

STEP 1: BRAINSTORM A THEME

The first step on the path to making a movie is to come up with a topic, theme, or idea from some existing footage that you want to turn into a movie. If you're like most people, you have footage on your video camera that you took during a recent trip, on your last vacation, or while you were just playing around the house. This footage probably doesn't have any consistent theme or idea but is just a collection of people, places, and events you thought were cool. However, with a little thought, you can come up with a topic from that footage that would make a good two-minute movie. Think of something you can use from your footage that could be pulled together for your first project.

The example used in this chapter was taken on a vacation in Maui in April 2003. One of the activities on the trip was taking a trip on a whale-watching boat. As you'd expect, there was plenty of video footage taken on that trip, as well as video and digital pictures of other vacation activities. A two-minute movie about whale-watching activities is perfect for this project!

STEP 2: GATHER ALL YOUR PIECES

The next step involves gathering all the pieces of information you think will go into your movie. These are called source files, and they're the video clips, still images, music files, audio files, and other files you want to use in your movies. A file is considered a source file if it's on your computer or is in a format that can be imported onto your computer. You can capture video files from your camcorder, download them from the Internet, or copy them from a VCR. You can use still images from your digital camera, from your scanner, from your artwork in Photoshop, from the Internet, or from a friend as an attachment to an e-mail. Music files typically will come from CDs. And your audio files might be narrations that you recorded or sound effects from the Internet.

The Maui vacation produced more than enough material. There was more than two-and-a-half hours of video footage, but as you'd expect with whales, where you aim the camcorder isn't where the whale will emerge, so most of the footage was of water. Getting some actual whale video footage was a bit of luck, but there were several shots of whales and whale tails that could be used from the original footage. There was also a CD with about 600 still pictures from the trip. Very few of them were of whales.

For audio, some video contained the tour guide's narration on the sound track. There was also some video from inside a hotel with lounge music in the background. These audio clips would be good raw material for the audio track.

In hindsight this might seem obvious, but it's easy to forget when you're in the middle of filming: camcorders record audio as well as video. If the noises and sounds around you are interesting, let the camcorder record the background noise even if the visuals are boring. By using Movie Maker, you can employ the audio track from your video footage elsewhere in your movie.

STEP 3: IMPORT YOUR IMAGES

Once you've identified all the source files that will go into making your movie, the next step is to import them into Movie Maker. Video files must be either captured from a video device, such as a camcorder, or imported from an existing video file, such as an MPG or WMV file. You can import other sources, such as pictures or songs, directly into Movie Maker from existing files.

WHAT MAKES A GOOD MOVIE SOURCE?

While you collect clips for your movies, at some point you'll want to add clips from other sources. Movie Maker 2 can use or import videos from several video and audio sources, but it isn't a universal editing environment. If you want to use footage from other movies, you'll need to make sure all your potential source files are usable in Movie Maker 2.

Say, for example, you want to use old movie clips for your new movie, and those movie clips were created using different software. Some other movie software formats such as Apple QuickTime movies (those with the .mov extension) aren't in a suitable format for Movie Maker. You must first convert the source file by saving the original file in a format recognized by Movie Maker or by using other software that converts between formats for you.

So when you collect your favorite pieces of music, digital images, or movies, be aware that you might need to take a couple extra steps before you can work with them directly in Movie Maker. The following are some places to find more information and instructions:

- For a list of what video and audio formats Movie Maker supports, see Chapter 4.

- For help importing footage from a VCR or a TV tuner card, see Chapter 7.

- If you want to turn all those old Super-8 movies into digital video, see Chapter 7.

- For general discussions about importing files, finding links to image and movie sites, and using other software for converting files, visit *http://www. papajohn.org*.

Write down a list of what you want to include in your movie, and then go get the original source materials. If you have video footage from particular tapes you want to use, get your camcorder and tapes ready to go. If you have digital pictures on a CompactFlash card, pull the camera and the memory card out of the closet where you left them after your last trip. Make scans of pictures, and rip songs from CDs. Don't worry if you don't know all the items you need; the great advantage of nonlinear editing using Movie Maker is that, if you think of something later, you can easily go back and add it.

The example in this chapter walks you through capturing video from a digital video device, importing still pictures, and importing sound. You'll use these source files to create your first movie.

CAPTURING FROM A VIDEO DEVICE

This example uses a FireWire capture card, a FireWire cable, and a camcorder with a FireWire connection. Analog devices use a slightly different process but can also capture video images. See Chapter 7 for information on using analog camcorders or other capturing devices. To capture from a video device, follow these steps:

1. Start Movie Maker 2 and open the Movie Tasks pane by clicking the Tasks button on the toolbar.

2. Connect the FireWire cable to your computer and to the camcorder.

3. Turn on the camcorder, and set the switch to VCR or VTR. This puts the camcorder in video playback mode. If your camcorder is already properly connected and turned on, you can launch the Video Capture Wizard by clicking Capture From Video Device in the Movie Tasks list.

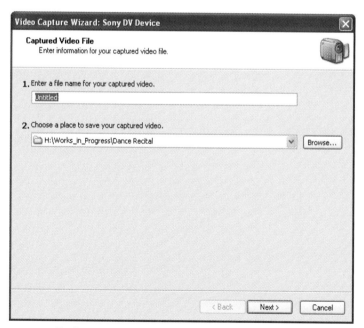

Figure 1-7 The Captured Video File dialog box is where you enter the name and location for your file.

④ If a dialog box appears asking you which application to use, choose Movie Maker 2.

⑤ Choose a name and hard disk folder for the captured video source file. You can create a folder for each project on your hard disk and then save all your files to that folder. If you're feeling really organized, create separate subfolders for each type of source file and save your video captures in the appropriate folder. You should give your files topical or informative names rather than dates or device names; this makes it easier to tell what the file contains. Figure 1-7 shows you the dialog box when you save a video capture file. When ready, click Next.

⑥ Select a video quality setting for your source file. This setting determines the video source quality vs. the file size it takes up on your computer. Figure 1-8 shows you the choices available. Although you might be tempted to go with the Movie Maker recommendation of Best Quality For Playback On My Computer (Recommended), for the purposes of this exercise select Digital Device Format. Chapter 4 covers video quality for different types of playback in more detail.

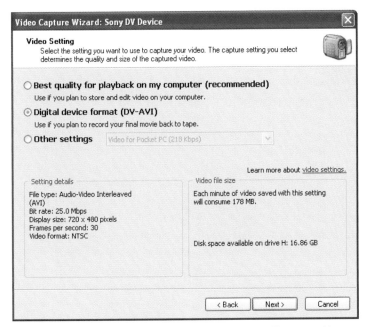

Figure 1-8 The Video Setting dialog box lets you select the trade-offs between video quality and file size on your computer.

7 Select the video capture method. The Capture Method dialog box shown in Figure 1-9 offers you the choice of automatically capturing the whole tape, which is typically one hour for a digital video camcorder, or of manually selecting the sections of the tape you want. If you have the disk space, which for DV-AVI quality is about 12–13 gigabytes (GB) per hour of source tape, you can record the whole tape automatically. For this exercise, select Capture Parts Of The Tape Manually.

The check box at the bottom of the screen cautions you about previewing during the capture session, which possibly affects the quality of the captured file. But even with an older 866 megahertz (MHz) computer, there were no problems during capture sessions for this example with the preview running. If your captures have dropped frames or have "skips" in them, rerun the wizard but without the video preview option. Click Next to move on to the next step of the wizard.

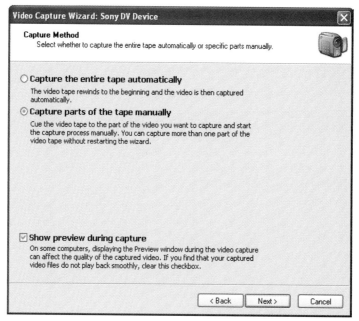

Figure 1-9 The Capture Method dialog box lets you select between automatic or manual capture.

8. Select your capture segments by using the controls under the wizard's monitor to get the tape to where you want to start a capture. Then back up a few seconds before the beginning of the clip to ensure you don't miss even one frame of the important video footage, and click the Start Capture button. Figure 1-10 shows you the capture process in action.

   Some camcorders support the computer being able to control the camcorder's playback VCR functions. For those that don't, you'll have to do the starting and stopping on the camcorder itself instead of using the video capture controls in Movie Maker. Click the Start Capture button in Movie Maker, and then press the Play button on the camcorder.

9. Start and stop the capture as you want. The data in the wizard will tell you how much hard disk space has been used so far and how much is left on the disk on which you're creating the new file. Movie Maker will create clips when the wizard finishes while it imports the source file into your collection bin.

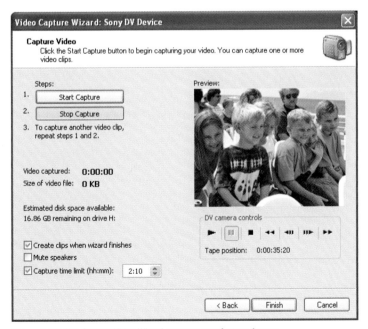

Figure 1-10 The Capture Video Wizard captures your footage for you.

⑩ Setting a time limit for capturing is a good idea. If the video segment you're capturing is eight minutes, then tell Movie Maker to stop the process automatically after eight minutes to let the capture process work without constant monitoring. The capture process is in real time. If you have 60 minutes of video, it'll take 60 minutes to capture. You can't speed it up to finish more quickly, and you can't slow it down to get higher quality.

⑪ When you've finished your capturing, click the Finish button, and the wizard will copy the temporary file to the final one in your chosen folder, using the filename you selected earlier. Figure 1-11 shows the progress meter as the file importing is done. Movie Maker 2 will create a new collection with the same name as the source file and put the new clip or clips into it. It'll place the new collection into your collection tree in alphabetical order with your existing collections.

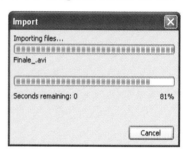

The importing isn't finished until the bottom bar reaches 100%. Let the wizard finish and close the window automatically.

Figure 1-11 Monitoring the progress meter during video importing

IMPORTING STILL IMAGES

It's easy to import still images into your collection for use in a movie. Still images can be anything from snapshots taken with a digital camera to scanned photos and slides to pictures and illustrations from the Internet. To import still images, follow these steps:

① Create a new collection in the Collections pane by right-clicking the Collections icon, selecting New Collection, typing a new name, and then clicking OK. You can also select an existing collection icon for your image clips.

② Click File | Import into Collections. Browse to the folder where you keep the images you want to import.

③ Select one or more images, and click Import.

The images will go into the collection as one image per file. By default Movie Maker displays images with a thumbnail picture of each file. When you select an image, you can view it in the Monitor pane.

You can also make still images from frames of imported video clips using the Monitor pane. To do this, follow these steps:

1 Slide the seek bar under the monitor or the playback indicator on the timeline to the frame you want to capture as a still image.

2 Click the Take Picture button on the monitor.

3 Type a filename for your still image, and click Save.

This saves the image to your computer and imports it into the collection you've selected.

IMPORTING AUDIO

Importing audio tracks or audio files is identical to the process used for still images. As with still images, the audio tracks need to be files on your computer before you can import them into Movie Maker. You can use Windows Media Player or other audio software to capture audio tracks.

When you import video, still images, audio clips, and other media into Movie Maker, it doesn't create copies of your files. Instead, the source files stay in their original locations on your hard disk. If you rename or move a source file, the thumbnail will show a big red X instead of the normal image. Select the clip you want to use and right-click it, and you'll have an option to browse for the "missing" file and repoint Movie Maker to it.

TIP

STEP 4: PREVIEW, SPLIT, AND COMBINE CLIPS

Now that you've assembled some video footage, some still images, and some music or audio tracks, it's time to review the video footage and identify likely candidates for your two-minute movie. Movie Maker lets you switch between thumbnails and details of your clips so you can select the right clip for the movie. Once you have a clip selected, you can preview the clip in the Monitor pane to see if it contains useful footage for your project. If the clip is too big, you can make smaller clips out of larger clips. For example, you captured eight minutes of video from your camera but want to have a clip for each time you started and stopped the recording. Movie Maker lets you split the larger clip into smaller ones.

SWITCHING BETWEEN VIEWS

You can switch between Thumbnails view and Details view for your imported clips. The Thumbnails view is great when you're looking around for an appropriate image or clip, but you're limited to seeing only the thumbnail and the clip name. The Details view shows the clip's name, duration, starting time in the tape, ending time, pixel dimensions, and date/time. The Details view is great when you're searching for a clip that has a specific duration and that you need in a particular place in your movie. To switch between views, follow these steps:

1. Click View.

2. Click either Thumbnails or Details.

The view changes to the one you selected. Figure 1-12 shows the Collections pane in Details view.

Collection: 29D - Boarding and Dolphins
Drag a clip and drop it on the timeline below.

Name	Duration	St...	End Time	Dimensions	Date Taken
Dock and Boats	0:00:25	0:05:31	0:05:57	320 x 240	4/18/2003 4:25 PM
People on Dock	0:00:32	0:05:57	0:06:28	320 x 240	4/18/2003 4:25 PM
Boarding	0:00:33	0:06:28	0:07:01	320 x 240	4/18/2003 4:25 PM
Other Boats	0:00:39	0:07:01	0:07:40	320 x 240	4/18/2003 4:25 PM
Bernadette Taking Pix	0:00:15	0:07:40	0:07:55	320 x 240	4/18/2003 4:25 PM
Looking for Whales	0:00:28	0:07:55	0:08:23	320 x 240	4/18/2003 4:25 PM
Boat - Group	0:00:22	0:08:23	0:08:45	320 x 240	4/18/2003 4:25 PM
29D (3)	0:00:39	0:08:45	0:09:24	320 x 240	4/18/2003 4:25 PM
29D (2)	0:02:34	0:09:24	0:11:58	320 x 240	4/18/2003 4:25 PM
Spinner Dolphin and Boat	0:00:35	0:11:58	0:12:33	320 x 240	4/18/2003 4:25 PM
29D (4)	0:00:12	0:12:33	0:12:45	320 x 240	4/18/2003 4:25 PM
Dolphins and Spinner	0:00:17	0:12:45	0:13:01	320 x 240	4/18/2003 4:25 PM
Boat and Dolphins	0:00:38	0:13:01	0:13:40	320 x 240	4/18/2003 4:25 PM
29D (5)	0:00:24	0:13:40	0:14:04	320 x 240	4/18/2003 4:25 PM
Nice Dolphins with Our Boat	0:00:14	0:14:04	0:14:18	320 x 240	4/18/2003 4:25 PM
Dolphins With Our Boat	0:00:20	0:14:18	0:14:38	320 x 240	4/18/2003 4:25 PM
Watching	0:00:04	0:19:10	0:19:14	320 x 240	4/18/2003 4:25 PM
Whales - 2	0:00:10	0:19:14	0:19:24	320 x 240	4/18/2003 4:25 PM
Whale Body	0:00:21	0:21:00	0:21:21	320 x 240	4/18/2003 4:25 PM
Tails and Spouts	0:00:39	0:21:21	0:22:00	320 x 240	4/18/2003 4:25 PM
29D (1)	0:00:54	0:22:30	0:23:24	320 x 240	4/18/2003 4:25 PM
Nice Tail	0:00:10	0:23:24	0:23:34	320 x 240	4/18/2003 4:25 PM
29D (7)	0:01:27	0:23:34	0:25:01	320 x 240	4/18/2003 4:25 PM
Big Nice Tail	0:00:23	0:25:01	0:25:24	320 x 240	4/18/2003 4:25 PM
Bodies	0:02:24	0:25:24	0:27:48	320 x 240	4/18/2003 4:25 PM
29D (6)	0:01:43	0:27:48	0:29:30	320 x 240	4/18/2003 4:25 PM
Big and Close Tail	0:00:10	0:29:30	0:29:40	320 x 240	4/18/2003 4:25 PM
29D (9)	0:02:58	0:29:40	0:32:38	320 x 240	4/18/2003 4:25 PM
Whale and Start of Good Narrative	0:00:59	0:32:38	0:33:37	320 x 240	4/18/2003 4:25 PM
More Narrative	0:01:20	0:33:37	0:34:57	320 x 240	4/18/2003 4:25 PM
Nice Tail	0:00:26	0:34:57	0:35:23	320 x 240	4/18/2003 4:25 PM
Heads and Bodies	0:00:22	0:35:23	0:35:45	320 x 240	4/18/2003 4:25 PM
Two Tails - Almost	0:00:47	0:37:25	0:38:12	320 x 240	4/18/2003 4:25 PM
Narrative Toward End	0:03:07	0:38:12	0:41:20	320 x 240	4/18/2003 4:25 PM
Heads, Bodies, Tails	0:01:20	0:41:20	0:42:39	320 x 240	4/18/2003 4:25 PM

Figure 1-12
Using the Collections pane in Details view

You can also change views either by right-clicking between clips in the Collections pane and then clicking the appropriate view or by clicking the Views button in the toolbar and clicking the appropriate view. Practice doing this a couple times to see how your clips look in each view.

PREVIEWING CLIPS

To preview a clip, select the clip you want to view in the Collections pane. The clip's first frame will appear in the monitor with the seek bar at the beginning of the clip. Note that the time figures under the monitor to the right are the location of the seek bar within the clip and the total length of the clip. The time is in hours, minutes, seconds, and 100ths of a second. Some video editing applications use frame numbers for the last number and not 100ths of a second. Movie Maker 2 is a 15-frames-per-second editing environment. If you preview a clip and move one frame at a time to the left or right, you'll see that it takes 15 frames to go exactly one second.

From left to right, you use the playback controls under the monitor to play or pause the clip, stop the preview and return to the zero position, go back to the zero position, go back one frame from the paused position, go forward one frame from the paused position, or go to the last frame of the clip. Play a clip or two in the monitor to get used to the Movie Maker playback controls.

SPLITTING AND COMBINING CLIPS

You can review the clips you imported into your collections and manually split them into the smaller ones you prefer. If you want to combine two or more smaller clips back into one longer clip, you can do that too, provided they're from the same source file and you haven't deleted any clips between them. To split a clip, follow these steps:

1. Select the clip in the collection you want to split.

2. Use the seek bar under the monitor to go to the desired split point within the clip. Drag it quickly to get close to a split point, and then use the controls to move left or right one frame at a time until you are where you want to split the clip.

3. Click the split clip button to split the large clip into two smaller clips. Movie Maker will leave the first part of the clip with the original name and make a second clip with the same name but with an additional numbered suffix.

To combine two or more clips, select the clips you want to combine, right-click, and then select Combine. This rejoins the clips into one longer clip.

Experiment with splitting and combining clips using one of your imported video clips to see how Movie Maker handles the splitting and combining tasks. If you have footage you'd like to use from your larger clips in your movie, feel free to make the smaller clips at this time.

At any time you can rename a clip to a sensible name for your project rather than use the automatically generated names. Select the clip and use the F2 key to quickly and easily rename it; just type the new name for your clip in the Collections pane, and press Enter. Your clip has been renamed.

STEP 5: CREATE A GREAT INTRODUCTION

Are you ready to begin the truly fun part of making a movie? Steps 5 through 7 are all about letting your creative side play with the clips you've assembled. The best part about this process is that you can keep moving clips around, adjusting the settings, or tweaking the duration of clips until it feels right to you. There are no mistakes because it's so easy to remove and add clips. If you don't like the way something looks, take out the parts you don't like and add the ones you do.

For your first project, two minutes might not have seemed like a long time initially. The average length of a TV commercial is 30 seconds, and if you don't capture a viewer's attention in 10 seconds, you risk boring them. Mention "home movies," and you might lose them before they see the first frame. After all, how often have you had unedited video footage forced on you by well-meaning friends and relatives? What makes your project instantly better than your neighbor's attempts at home video is that you have the tools to tell a story and the ability to hook their interest from the start. It's amazing what a few elements such as an introduction, a theme or story, smooth audio, and transitions can do!

For your two-minute movie, you don't need a long introduction. For almost any movie, your introduction should be no longer than 30 seconds. If you put together a shorter introduction that feels right, you can stop—you don't need to make it longer. For more information on "speaking" in your movie, see Chapter 3.

ADDING A STILL IMAGE

Go through the still images, either ones you imported or ones you made from your video footage, and find one that fits your general theme. It doesn't have to be the most spectacular picture you have or one of the biggest highlights of your trip. You can choose just about anything: a picture of all your suitcases next to the car; a wrong-way sign; one of your children, half in shadow, looking out a window; a setting sun; a picture from a museum. You can even harvest images from the Internet if there are ones you think would make a good starting image. Remember, the idea is to just get started, so it doesn't have to be perfect the first time around. You can always change the image later if you find one you like better.

The next step is to add your image to the storyboard. This is the easiest and best part of all. It's best to work with the storyboard when you first start out because in many ways it's easier to see what you're doing and get a good feel for your project when you work with the storyboard. If you're more comfortable working with the timeline, you can work there; but for this exercise, start with the storyboard.

To add an image to the storyboard, follow these steps:

1. If you're in Timeline view, click View Storyboard.

2. Scroll through your Collections pane until you find the image you want to use.

3. Click and drag the image to the storyboard. It'll go into the first large square at the left.

Your image appears in the storyboard as a thumbnail with the image name just below it. The Monitor pane shows your image in a larger size. If you have trouble seeing the images in the storyboard, click and drag the horizontal divider line up and down to resize the storyboard and its images. Figure 1-13 shows you the storyboard with two images added.

Figure 1-13 Adding two images to the storyboard

Now let's see how your work looks so far. To play the movie you've built to this point, follow these steps:

1. Click the first image in the storyboard.

2. Click the Play button in the Monitor pane.

Your images will play back, and the storyboard will highlight each successive image while the movie plays. By default, images last five seconds. You can change this setting easily, but for now the idea is to get the images in place. Fine-tuning will come later.

You can add as many still images as you want that help establish the location, the theme, or the mood you want to give your viewers. If it feels like there are too many images, you can remove images by right-clicking an image and then clicking Delete. This removal method works for everything in the storyboard or timeline.

If at any point you want to scrap the whole project and start over, you can clear the storyboard by pressing Ctrl+Delete. This removes everything from the storyboard: images, clips, audio, overlays, transitions, and effects. Make sure you really want to remove everything before using this command. Many times it's easier to take out the images or effects you don't want by using the Undo button to "back out" your changes than to start from scratch. Try undoing your changes before you decide to follow a scorched-earth policy and rebuild your movie entirely.

ADDING A SHORT INTRO CLIP

If you want, you can add a short clip instead of a still image. Just like still images, your introductory clip can be anything that helps set the topic or idea in a viewer's mind. If your still image depicted suitcases outside your car, the short clip could be footage of your family at the airport, waving at the camera as any tourist would. Or it could be a clip of a hotel sign, a freeway exit, or your tour guide. You can use any-thing to help hook your viewers and get them interested in what's to come.

You add video clips to the storyboard the same way you did with still images: find the clip you want, and then drag it to the storyboard. If you're looking for short clips, you can either switch to Details view to see the clip duration or hover your mouse over a video clip for a few seconds. A ToolTip appears that lists the clip's duration and filename.

Feel free to check your progress by playing your movie back. If the movie feels choppy, don't worry. You'll add transitions in later chapters.

ADDING A TEXT CLIP

A text clip is text that appears at the start of an image or video clip, between clips, or over the top of a clip. This includes elements such as opening titles, closing credits, or any text you want to appear anywhere in your movie. Using Movie Maker, you can change the font, the font color, the duration, and the overlay effects such as moving from left to right. You can put nearly anything on text clips; you're limited only by your imagination and the text visibility when you play back your movie.

For your introduction, the simpler, the better: a simple title screen at the beginning will tell your viewers what your movie is about. In keeping with your topic, think of what you'd like to see: "Family Vacation 2003" is great. So is "Trainspotting in Europe." Anything short and to the point will be easier to see when you make your movie, so go for short, snappy phrases rather than thesis-sized statements.

To add a title screen, follow these steps:

1. Click Tools | Titles And Credits.

2. Click Add Title At The Beginning Of The Movie.

3. Type your title into the box. While you type, your title will appear in the Monitor pane. By default, your title will be in white letters on a blue background. If you need to force a line break, you can do so by pressing Enter; otherwise the text will wrap automatically for you on the title screen.

4. Click Done | Add Title To Movie.

Now play your introduction. Your title has a duration of a few seconds and fades in and out, just like a professional credit sequence. In Chapter 2 you'll go through the process of editing various settings for the text overlay.

By now you should have the visual elements of your introduction in place. Remember, you don't need to force the introduction to be 30 seconds long; whatever feels right is exactly the length it should be.

ADDING AN AUDIO TRACK

You might have noticed that your introduction is pretty quiet unless you added a video clip containing audio to the storyboard. When you add still images and video clips to the storyboard, the video clips have their associated audio tracks, but the still pictures will have a resounding silence. To help draw your viewers into your movie, it's best to have an audio/music track running throughout your introduction and through the rest of the movie. It provides continuity to the visuals, and if a great audio source is used, it really enhances the movie presentation for the viewer. At this stage of the project, getting something half right in the timeline is enough. It's easy to change later when the project takes shape.

When you look at the storyboard, you won't see any obvious way to add audio to your movie. This is the first occasion where working with the timeline is more powerful than working with the storyboard. The storyboard is great for managing the visual aspects of your movie, but if you want to work with all the different parts that go into a movie, you need to switch to the timeline. It's there that you can add and remove audio tracks as easily as you did still images and video clips.

If you aren't in Timeline view already, click the Show Timeline button. The lower pane switches to the timeline, and you'll see three horizontal tracks: Video, Audio/Music, and Title Overlay. Figure 1-14 shows Movie Maker in Timeline view. Above the three tracks are time markings that you can use as reference points and a mini-toolbar to the upper left. At this point you won't need to use these buttons, but you'll work with them in later chapters.

If you've been following the exercise so far, you should have your title screen, still images, and video clip in the Video track. Now it's time to add an audio clip:

1. Browse through your collection of clips to find either an audio-only file or a video file that contains audio you want to use.

2. Click and drag the file to the start of the Audio/Music track.

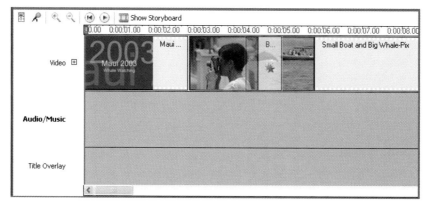

Figure 1-14 Using the Timeline view

This automatically adds the file containing audio to the project. You should see the audio clip's title and a visual "audiograph" of your clip in the Audio/Music track. Go ahead and test your movie by clicking the Play button. Doesn't that make your movie come alive? If the audio clip you added is longer than your introduction (or even longer than the two-minute length of your movie), don't worry about it. You'll trim and fine-tune your project in Chapter 2. You now have the first draft of your introduction. It's a good beginning, and while you work through the exercises in later chapters, it will get better.

STEP 6: ADD CLIPS TO THE BODY

Now that you've spent some time getting the introduction into shape, switch to the Storyboard view so you can create the body of your movie. Go through the clips in the Collections pane, dragging and dropping those that might work well in your movie. Keep in mind your general topic or idea, and rearrange the clips so they follow an order that matches your theme. If you're telling the story of your vacation, then chronological order is great for keeping the story in a nice, linear form. If you're telling the story of museums you visited, you don't have to go in chronological order; you can mix and match by painters, by schools of art, or even by theme or mood.

You can also include happy accidents by mixing together scenes that bring laughter or add a humorous counterpoint to your main story. In a museum story, for instance, you can mix together shots of important artwork with "reaction shots" from your children taken from elsewhere on your vacation or even from other vacations. Old Masters oil paintings? Yawn. Postmodern sculpture? Frown. Almost-naked classical statuary? Big grin.

PUTTING CLIPS IN ORDER

Drag your clips to the storyboard, moving them left and right to change the sequence. Think about the flow of the movie project, and play it back to see how the parts fit together and to get the clips into the right part. In the example in Figure 1-15, there are 18 potential movie clips added to form the body.

In the example shown, after much judicious selection, the body clips are five clips of boarding the boat and going out to the whales, three clips of a surprise visit by dolphins, one clip of people on the boat looking for the whales, six of the nicer whale clips (mostly tails because the nicer head shots were used for stills in the introduction), and three clips of the boat and scenery heading back to shore. Once the sequencing is done, it is back to the Timeline view. For this example, you need to cut down the overall time to fit the two-minute guideline.

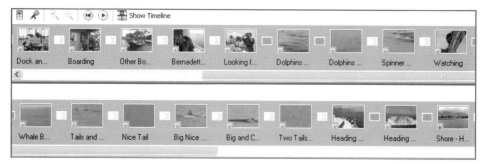

Figure 1-15 Using the storyboard with 18 movie clips added

ADJUSTING TRIM POINTS

One of the big advantages of working with clips in the timeline rather than working with clips in the Collections pane is the ability to trim the clip within the project. Unlike splitting a clip, which divides clips into two parts with all of the frames visible in each clip, trimming a clip allows you to hide some frames at the beginning or end of the clip. When you set trim points, you set a start trim point somewhere after the beginning of the clip and an end trim point somewhere before the end. That way, only the frames between the start trim point and end trim point will play. The remaining frames aren't discarded but are "hidden." The hidden frames remain with the clip in the timeline, and you can readjust the trim point locations at any time during your editing. This lets you choose which part of the clip plays in your movie, without requiring you to physically split a clip every time you want to change which parts of it play.

This sounds tricky but is much easier to do than it sounds. To set a trim point in the timeline, follow these steps:

1. Select the clip you want to trim.

2. Move the cursor to the beginning or end of the clip. A double-headed red arrow appears.

3. Click and drag the mouse to trim the clip.

The clip is shaded to show the visible part of the clip, and the playback indicator moves to show where the trim point will be set. A ToolTip appears, showing you the clip's name and the trimmed clip's duration. When you release the mouse, the clip shrinks to fit its new size, and the rest of the clips in the timeline adjust accordingly—no gaps are left when you trim a clip.

Figure 1-16 uses a clip from the whale-watching trip. The clip is being trimmed to show only the part when the whale's tail appears and disappears in the water.

If you need finer control over setting a trim point in your clip, follow these steps:

1. Use either the monitor's seek bar or the playback indicator on the timeline to move to the specific frame you want to use as a trim point.

2. Click Clip from the drop-down menu.

3. If you're setting a start trim point, click Set Start Trim Point. If you're setting an end trim point, click Set End Trim Point.

In addition to the clip handles that appear when you select the clip, there will also be gray areas on the time scale. These gray areas indicate the trimmed parts of the selected clip that are hidden by the current trim point settings. If there are no gray areas at either end of the clip, there are no frames hidden by the trim points. If you set a start trim point on the timeline's first clip, there won't be a gray area on the left end. The clip's hidden frames are off the scale to the left of the timeline, but it's the only clip in the project that works that way.

Preview your movie, and adjust the trim points to show only those parts of your clips that help tell the story. Preview again and adjust some more so that each clip shows only the scenes you want to show and for the duration that feels right to you. Take advantage of the wonderfully easy way to set and adjust the trim points. In the example shown, the 20 minutes or more of video clips that were selected were easily trimmed to get down to around the two-minute mark.

FINDING JUST THE RIGHT SOUND

Once your video selection feels right, you can focus on the audio. You can adjust the audio clips in the same manner because Movie Maker lets you set trim points for the audio clips. Remember that you can mix and match audio clips from different video clips; if you have some great ambient background sounds from one video clip, you can use the clip as background for your other video clips. No one will know that the audio and video were not shot simultaneously!

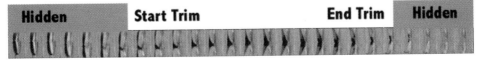

Figure 1-16 Trimming a clip to show only the whale's tail

One feature to watch for: the audio/music clips do not behave quite the same way when you set trim points. If you shrink down an audio clip, the other clips don't move together and automatically close the gap. You might need to move the clips manually so that you have continuous audio running during your video.

In the whale-watching movie, a single audio clip was used for 10 of the video clips. Because most of the trimmed clips were action shots of whales, it was easy to include a single audio track of the other passengers from a different video clip during some dramatic whale-watching moments.

STEP 7: CREATE AN ENDING

By now you have an introduction and middle that runs somewhere around two minutes, more or less. You're nearly done! All that remains to finish your movie is an ending.

Because you're now familiar with your video clips and still images, you should identify one that helps you finish telling your story. Something that brings the video full circle or indicates the end of a journey is a worthwhile ending. For your ending, you can use a clip that you've been saving as an exclamation point in your movie. Or you can create closing credits or titles that display over background music. A still picture with audio of your family saying "Wow, what a great vacation!" works just fine. Anything that helps your viewers feel you've ended the story will work.

For the example in this chapter, the introduction is fairly long, and given that this is a two-minute movie, there isn't much time left for an ending. So in this case, simpler is better: just add a title overlay to say goodbye in some way. For now it acts as a space filler and movie closer, and later editing sessions will explore some other techniques that can help close a movie.

STEP 8: SAVE YOUR MOVIE

Up until now you've been saving your project files between editing sessions and viewing your movie in the monitor. The monitor has been showing you a preview of what the movie will look like, but it's not the actual finished movie. The process of making a movie file from your project is called rendering. When you render a movie, Movie Maker builds it piece by piece from your source files and puts them together using the movie settings in your project file.

Rendering takes a lot of time and computer processing power. Even with a powerful computer, it might take two to three times the playing time of the movie to render the movie file. Most of the computer's energy will be devoted to the rendering process, slowing it down for other tasks. You can continue to use the computer for instant messaging and e-mail while the rendering takes place, but in many cases you'll probably be happier taking a break to stretch your legs and get the cricks out of your back. When the rendering is finished, Movie Maker will copy the newly created movie file to the folder you selected on your computer.

Although you can render a movie for a number of different devices, for now the example will render a file for your PC. Other destinations will be explored in later chapters, including DVDs.

To save your project as a movie file, follow these steps:

1 Click File | Save Movie File.

2 In the Save Movie Wizard, the first option is highlighted. It saves your movie in your selected folder on the hard disk. Click Next.

3 Type a filename for your movie. You can use any character to name your movie except \ / : * ? " < > or |. Fortunately, you don't have to remember these because Movie Maker will tell you if you try to use one of them. Figure 1-17 shows you the Saved Movie File dialog box.

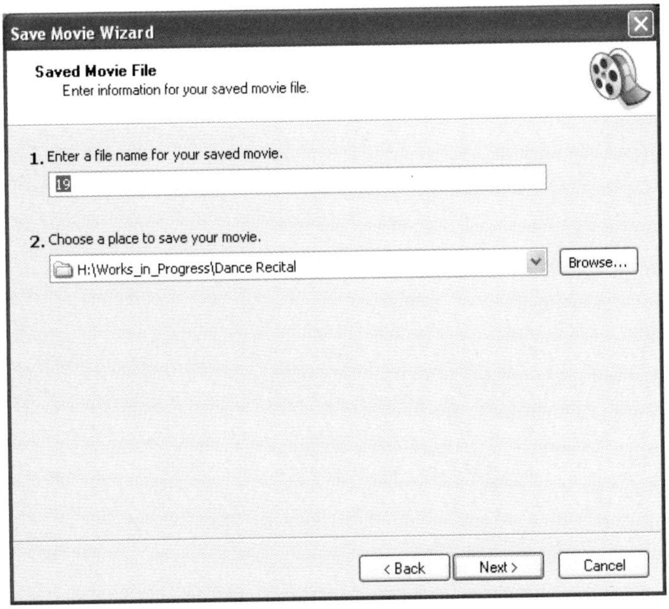

Figure 1-17 Specifying the location in the Saved Movie File dialog box

④ Browse to the folder you want to use for your finished movie. You can use the My Videos folder, or you can browse to the project folder if you created one earlier. Once you've selected it, click Next.

⑤ Figure 1-18 shows the Movie Setting dialog box. If this is the first time you've run the wizard, the only choice visible might be Best Quality For Playback On My Computer (Recommended). The dialog box also shows the settings for movie setting and file size. This is your last chance, so if you have second thoughts or don't want to render at this time, click Cancel. For now, no changes are needed, so click Next.

Movie Maker starts the rendering process and shows you a dialog box that indicates the estimated rendering time remaining and the percentage complete. When it's done, the last dialog box appears. Click Finish, and if you want, you can play your newly rendered movie by leaving the check box selected.

That's it! You've finished your first amazing project using Movie Maker. Your movie is now automatically better than 99 percent of all other home movies, thanks to your time spent using Movie Maker. Congratulations!

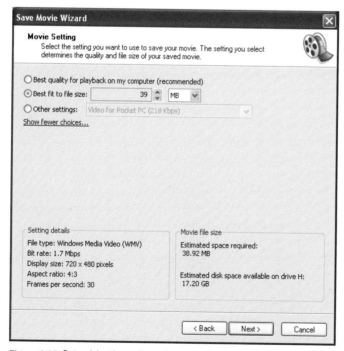

Figure 1-18 Determining the quality and size using the Movie Setting dialog box

SUMMER VACATION MOVIES: GET THE FULL FAMILY PERSPECTIVE

Movie Maker 2 can be a springboard for all kinds of entertaining projects that you can put together, simply using your creativity and an hour or two of your time. But why let the fun stop at just individual projects? Why not get others involved in the excitement of making movies?

No two people will create the same movie using the same source material. It might be interesting to see what type of movie someone else comes up with using your collection of clips, still images, and audio files. Or even more interesting, how would the same activity look from someone else who participated in that activity? What if you decided to turn the keyboard and mouse over to the people closest to you, such as the ones who traveled with you on your last vacation? They'll have different perspectives of the vacation, and they'll have insights you might not have considered. It's a good way to see how different visions work with similar material and to have a laugh or two when wildly different "takes" on your vacation appear on your TV. In the end, you might combine some different perspectives into a movie that looks like this:

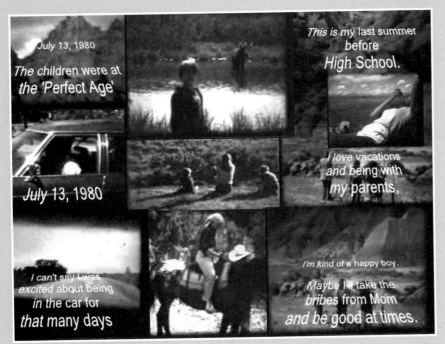

A different perspective from various family members on the same summer vacation

To launch this project, follow these steps:

1. Get everyone involved. In the best of all possible worlds, you give everyone a camcorder or digital camera before you go on vacation and tell them to go crazy. However, like most folks, you probably have only one camcorder or one camcorder and one digital camera for everyone to share. If that's the case, before you go on vacation or on a trip, tell everyone about your idea of having each person make their own movie and set up a schedule for "sharing" the camera or camcorder.

2. Keep a daily log or a diary of events. When professional photographers go on a shoot, they keep a log of what they shoot and when they shoot it so they can quickly identify relevant footage and subject matter. If you have many people using the same camera, you might want to designate one person as the keeper of the camera log—specifically, who shot what footage when. This will come in handy when you're importing footage later. It's also helpful for everyone to keep a journal or diary during the trip. It's always surprising how much detail you think you'll remember once you get home; you can easily "lose" it after only a couple months. These journals, combined with the camera log, will help everyone remember details that can be used later in the individual movies.

3. Launch your project. Everyone now has the task of "filming" your vacation. When you get back home, you'll all bring your raw material to the table and begin the work of creating the movie.

Once you have the raw material for the project, you can take some additional steps before getting everyone involved in the creative process. You can prepare your computer and your family for the upcoming movie-making project and give your family and friends a comfortable, convenient way to learn how to create their own movies.

To prepare your files for work on the computer, follow these steps:

1. Set up a common Movie Studio user account. The simplest way to provide access to imported video, still images, audio, and title materials is to set up a common account that everyone can use to create movies. Chapter 4 goes into detail about the benefits of having a shared Windows XP account for creating movies.

2. Give a short "training course" on Movie Maker to your friends and family. From this chapter, you've seen how easy it can be to create movies; now

you can share your knowledge. Show your friends or family members how to log on to Windows XP using the Movie Studio account, start Movie Maker, and then drag and drop clips, images, and sound to the storyboard or to the timeline. Most people find it easier to start with the storyboard and then switch to the timeline when needed for working with audio tracks and adjusting transition or effect properties.

3 Organize the source material. As you can see in the following graphic, it can be daunting to look through a long list of files...even when they have descriptive filenames. To make it easier for everyone, create folders or collections for your images. Organizing by date, city, landmark, or other easily remembered categories is a good way for everyone to find the source material quickly. For ideas on organizing your digital materials, see Chapter 4.

With these preparations in place, you're ready to start the eight-step process outlined in this chapter. Let the projects begin!

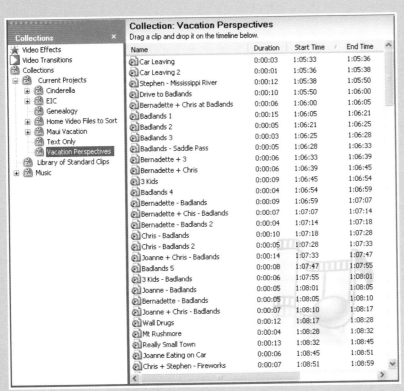

The Vacation Perspectives collection shows the list of generic clips that can be used by everyone on the project.

If you wanted, you could stop now, not learn another fact about Movie Maker, and continue turning out quality home movies to show others on your computer. But Movie Maker is capable of so much more. Learn how to turn your quality movies into amazing ones, learn how to distribute your movies, and learn what other effects you can create by using the tools you've explored so far. The following chapters in this part will go more into detail about the powerful abilities in Movie Maker. For instance, you'll learn about adding transitions between clips, adding special effects to your clips, doing more complex audio edits and editing enhancements, organizing your files and movies, and publishing your movie to CD, DVD, or even the Internet. Stick around for the other chapters to really take your movie-making skills to the next level.

Glossary

capture
To record audio, video, or a still image as a digital file on your computer's hard disk.

clips
For video only, a series of frames that contain a continuous action or scene. For Movie Maker in general, a clip is anything you see in a collection or on the timeline. Clips might be audio, video, narration, pictures, or text.

FireWire
Apple Computer's trademark name for a high-speed data streaming format. It is most commonly used with digital media devices such as camcorders and video capture cards.

frames
Single still images from a video clip.

import
To make a source file available for Movie Maker to use when you create a project. You aren't actually copying the source file into your project. Instead, information about the source file is added to the collection database.

project	Contains information about the clips used to make your movie, about how the clips are arranged, and about what transitions and effects are applied. Every movie you create is part of a project. Each movie has a unique project file that has the .MSWMM extension.
rendering	The process of building a movie from source files so that it can be viewed on another system, such as a PC or a DVD player.
source file	A file on your computer that contains an image, a clip, a soundtrack, or all the footage from your digital video camera.
storyboard	A graphical depiction of how a scene or movie will play. Historically storyboards were drawn by hand, much like comic strips, showing a director how a scene would be filmed.
text clip	Any text you see that was not filmed initially. This can be opening titles, closing credits, scene transitions, or even "silent movie" dialogue.
timeline	Uses a time scale that measures the length of clips within a scene and works in real time while the scene plays back.
trim points	Markers you set within a clip that tell Movie Maker which part of the clip to include in the final movie. Frames outside the trim points are "invisible" but are still available if you need to readjust the trim points during the editing process.

- **Unleash Your Creativity**
- **Use Transitions Effectively Between Clips**
- **Add Video Effects to Clips**
- **Use Effects with Still Pictures**
- **Create Amazing Text Effects**
- **Get Inspiration from an "Automatically" Created Movie**
- **Personalize Your Workspace**

Adding Flashy and Classy Video Effects

CHAPTER 2

Visual effects are the secret to making an amazing movie. By adding a few video effects to your movie, you elevate your movie from ordinary to extraordinary. Visual effects are one of the most notable ways you can distinguish your movie from a movie made by your friends, family, or even coworkers. Visual effects are also an expression of your creativity; your movie expresses who you are and shows off your creative eye for putting movies together. Given the same set of clips and Microsoft Windows Movie Maker 2 software, no two people will create the same story. Adding flashy and classy video effects is one of the easiest ways to pull your movie together, enhance its ability to tell a tale, and make it sing.

You can use animations to make your text be crazy or classy, depending on the mood you're setting.

Coming Attractions

When creativity is the key ingredient, it doesn't matter how many source files you have or what the quality of your clips is. Using video effects and transitions, you'll amaze yourself when you see your movie take on a professional look so quickly and easily. The best part of making a movie in Movie Maker 2 is seeing how fast it comes together and how rapidly you can change the look and feel just by using a few different transitions or effects on the clips you selected for your movie.

Unleash your creativity, and do anything you want to with your movie. Stop often to preview it while it develops, and use your intuition and imagination to make changes based on what you see. Try lots of features. Do your fine-tuning, bring music into the project, and add narrative and text. Laugh and smile while your movie takes shape. Let this be your time to play and stretch your wings and fly. Build your project by yourself until you're ready to do a prerelease or sneak preview for your friends and relatives. Then show them what you've done, perhaps ask them what they liked best, and maybe even show them how you go about creating a movie. When they see what you've done and how easy it is, they just might want to sit down and start making a movie too.

If your creative juices just aren't flowing, give yourself a break and stop that particular project for a while until you're ready to return. One good way to keep your perspective fresh is to work on a number of projects in parallel. Put one aside for a while, and open another and work on it. Change projects when your energy level changes. And remember that you can't goof up a project because every feature and every effect is changeable using a few mouse clicks. The only rule is that there are no rules. Anything goes!

If you've followed the exercises from Chapter 1, you have your first movie "in the can." Want to do even more with your movie and make it come alive? Then follow along with the suggestions in this chapter. It's all about expressing your creativity through video effects. Be prepared to dazzle your audience. You'll learn how to use transitions between clips and add video effects to specific clips to enhance your existing movies. You'll also learn more about some of the Movie Maker 2 options and video capture settings you can use to have greater creative control and flexibility over your projects. You'll also see how Movie Maker can quickly build a movie for you using the AutoMovie option. Using all these options, you'll be making movies that make it look like you've been doing it for years!

> Movie Maker uses generic Microsoft images when you preview a transition or effect in the monitor. If you want to use cooler pictures, such as ones of your family or favorite vacation spots instead, rename the pictures to Sample1.jpg and Sample2.jpg and copy them into the Program Files\Movie Maker\Shared folder.
>
> TIP

Dressing Up Your Video with Transitions

Video transitions are effects you apply to move between one clip and another. You can apply these transitions anywhere: between video clips, between a clip and an image, between titles or images, or between any combination you can create. With film, creating visual transitions is a complex and time-consuming process; using Movie Maker, it's as simple as dragging and dropping.

Video transitions can be simple or complex, and they can subtly enhance a mood or crash joyously into a picture. Transitions are often used in real-world slide shows, where they're very appropriate. They help make those presentations feel "alive," not static and dead. However, when you add transitions to movies, you have to be careful to strike an appropriate balance between subtlety and mind-numbing obviousness. Transitions can be so glaring that you might be pulling your viewer's attention away from the storyline. If you want your transitions to be the stars of your movie, that's fine—as long as that's what you intend to do. Play around with using transitions, and if they appear to be too much, then they probably are.

In Chapter 1, you worked with a transition when you created your first movie. A video transition called a simple cut was used, where the last frame of one clip was followed directly by the first frame of the next clip. Simple cuts are far-and-away the most common transition in movies or video of any kind. The next time you watch a movie, notice how often a simple cut moves from one scene to the next. This transition is used perhaps 90 percent of the time, and it's so common that audiences don't notice when it's used. It's also the default transition applied when you add video clips directly to a project.

The second most common transition is the cross-fade. With a cross-fade, the last frames of one clip fade, or dissolve, into the starting frames of the next. If you're keeping track of the transitions used in a movie, watch for how often cross-fades are used. They don't appear as often as simple cuts, but they're common enough that you'll recognize them immediately.

Working with transitions is simple using Movie Maker. You select a transition from the Video Transitions collection, drag it into the appropriate place in the storyboard or timeline, test the transition, and then change any transition properties to make your movie look right. It's an easy process and one that lets you try a number of different transitions before deciding on what looks right to you.

DISPLAYING AND PREVIEWING VIDEO TRANSITIONS

Your video transitions are stored in the Video Transitions collection. The collection displays each transition and a graphical representation of what each transition does. Downloading transitions from Microsoft at *http://www.microsoft.com/windowsxp/ moviemaker/default.asp*, or installing transitions from other software companies adds them to this collection.

Movie Maker gives you an easy way to preview how a transition will look. You can select and play a transition in the Monitor pane to see how it'll affect your clips. Figure 2-1 shows you a preview in action.

To display the Video Transitions collection and play a transition, follow these steps:

1 Click the Collections button on the toolbar until the Collections view is visible in the Tasks pane.

2 Click Video Transitions.

3 Scroll through the list of video transitions in the Contents pane.

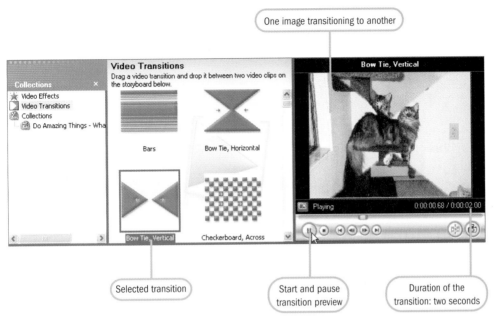

One image transitioning to another

Figure 2-1
The Monitor pane shows a preview of a selected video transition.

Selected transition

Start and pause transition preview

Duration of the transition: two seconds

④ Click a transition. A picture appears in the Monitor pane.

⑤ Click Play in the Monitor pane. The transition plays using two still images, showing you how it'll look in your movie.

Try playing with the various transitions to see how they behave. While you play with them, you might want to identify two or three you think will work with your movie.

ADDING A VIDEO TRANSITION TO YOUR MOVIE

When you add a video transition to your movie, it's added using either the Storyboard or the Timeline view. In the Storyboard view, transitions are added to the small square boxes between each of the clips. In the Timeline view, transitions are added to the Transition track immediately below the Video track. If you don't see the Transition track, click the plus sign next to the Video track to expand it and show the Transition track. It's usually easiest to add transitions to the storyboard and then make any adjustments to settings later using the timeline.

Working with transitions is as easy as working with clips:

- To apply a transition to your project, drag a transition from the Video Transitions collection and drop it between two adjacent clips.

- To replace a transition, drag the new transition onto the existing transition, and the existing one will be replaced. You don't need to delete the existing transition before applying the new one.

- To delete a transition, select it and press Delete.

TIP To add the same transition between all the video clips of a project, first select all clips in the storyboard. Then, right-click the desired transition, and click Add To Storyboard (or press Ctrl+D). This will apply it to all clips.

When you select a transition, think about each of the two clips involved. What's the focus point within each clip? Do the focus points share the same general area on the monitor, or are they in different locations? Depending on where the focus points are, you might be able to select from many transitions. In other cases, only a few transitions would work well.

Figure 2-2 shows a transition from the outside of a quaint old home to an indoor scene with two young girls. The eye transition was used because the girls' faces were fairly close to the center of the second clip, and the shape of the transition helped focus attention when moving from one clip to the next.

TESTING AND FINE-TUNING YOUR TRANSITIONS

Now you have a transition between two clips, so it's time to see how it looks while your movie runs. You can play back your clips and transition in two ways:

- If you're in the Storyboard view, click the clip just ahead of the transition. Then click the Play Storyboard button or the Play button on the Monitor pane.

- If you're in the Timeline view, click the Time track or slide the playback indicator to anywhere in the clip just ahead of the transition. Then click the Play Timeline button or the Play button on the Monitor pane.

Figure 2-2 An eye transition focuses the viewer's attention in the second clip.

The first clip begins playing. Your transition will occur toward the end of the first clip and slowly transition into the second clip. If you're in the Timeline view, you can see exactly when the transition begins and ends. If you don't like what the transition looks like between the two clips, try another one.

If you like the transition but it takes too long or isn't long enough, you can change the length of time it takes to move from one clip to another, also called the duration. You can set the duration by editing the transition in the timeline. If you're not already in the Timeline view, click the Show Timeline button. You'll see your transition on the Transition track, and you'll see a shaded area in the Video track where your two clips overlap. Transitions require some overlapping of the two adjacent clips. A selected transition shows a trim handle just like the video clip handles, but just on the one end that can be adjusted. The location of the trim point for the transition aligns with the location of the trim point of the associated video clip. As you move the transition, the preceding clip is shaded to show how much overlap occurs between the two clips. Figure 2-3 shows the duration editing process.

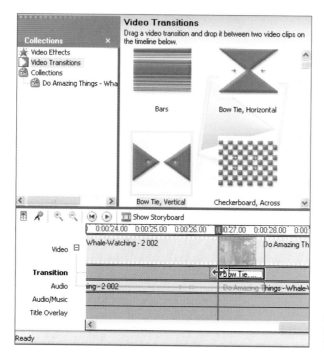

Figure 2-3 Adjust the transition duration by selecting and dragging the end of the duration.

To edit the transition's duration:

1 Select the transition.

2 Move the cursor to the beginning of the transition. A double-headed red arrow appears.

3 Click and drag the mouse to change the transition's duration.

If you want to know how much time the transition will take, you can hover your mouse over the transition. A ToolTip appears that shows you the transition name and its duration. Now play back your transition, and see how it changes the feel of your movie.

TIP
You can change the default transition duration in Movie Maker. Click Tools | Options, and then select the Advanced tab. Change the transition duration from 1.25 seconds to any duration you want. This will take effect on all newly added transitions but will not affect any transitions already in your project.

This is the point where your creativity kicks into gear. You'll be editing your clips' trim points and editing your transitions' durations to get the right balance and look for your movie. You'll work through a cycle of edit, adjust, play back, and then readjust. Once you think a transition is just about right, move to the next transition. Remember that you don't need a special transition between every clip; a simple cut will be enough most of the time. But when you want to change your film's tempo or indicate a change from one visual theme to another, you can explore various transitions to see which ones work best.

> You can easily add a fade transition by dragging a clip to overlap the previous one. Movie Maker automatically inserts a fade transition for you.

Spicing Up Your Clips with Video Effects

Video effects are special effects you apply to clips to enhance them or make them appear much different from the raw footage you captured on your camcorder. They're different from video transitions in two major ways. First, video transitions are used between clips, and video effects are used directly on the clips. Second, only one video transition at a time can be used between clips, but you can have up to six different video effects on a single clip. Or you can apply the same effect up to six times.

Your video effects are stored in the Video Effects collection. The collection displays each effect and a graphical representation of what each effect does. When you select the collection, you'll see the full set of 28 effects included with Movie Maker 2. If you download and install additional effects from Microsoft or from third-party suppliers, they'll be included in this collection.

Working with video effects is as easy as working with transitions. You select an effect, drag it to the storyboard or timeline, test the effect, and then make any changes to make the effect look right on the clip. Because you can stack effects on a clip or apply the same effect more than once, you can try a number of effects as well as change the effect order to see what works best for you.

DISPLAYING AND PREVIEWING VIDEO EFFECTS

Movie Maker gives you an easy way to preview a video effect. You can select and play an effect in the Monitor pane to see how it'll affect your clips. To display the Video Effects collection and play an effect, follow these steps:

1. Click the Collections button on the toolbar until the Collections view is visible in the Tasks pane.

2. Click the Video Effects folder (see Figure 2-4).

3. Scroll through the list of video effects in the Contents pane.

4. Click an effect. A picture appears in the Monitor pane.

5. Click Play in the Monitor pane. The effect plays using a single still image, showing you how it'll affect the clip in your movie.

Try playing with the various effects to see how they behave. While you play with them, you might get ideas on how to use them with specific clips.

EXPLORING THE TYPES OF VIDEO EFFECTS

You can organize the 28 effects in Movie Maker into several categories based on the effect they have on a clip.

Figure 2-4 The Video Effects folder contains all the effects you can apply to your clips.

Two effects, Ease In and Ease Out, gently zoom into or out of the clip, respectively, using the center of the clip as the point of focus. Use one of them when the clip's center of interest is somewhere close to the middle. These are nice to use on still pictures when you can crop the image to place the focus at the center, if it's not there already.

Two effects, Slow Down–Half and Speed Up–Double, produce slow motion or rapid clip speed. You can apply the same effect up to six times, so a clip that starts with a 10-second duration could be as short as 0.3 seconds or as long as 5 minutes and 20 seconds.

Six effects flip (Mirror, Vertical, or Horizontal) or rotate (Rotate 90, Rotate 180, and Rotate 270) a clip. Flipping clips helps move the composition by swapping the picture around; notice that if you use the Mirror–Horizontal effect, you'll reverse any text in your raw footage. Rotating clips also helps with composition by pivoting the clip around an imaginary center point. You can use this for better composition, such as for rotating clips of flowers or still pictures or even for compensating for filming a scene by holding the camcorder sideways.

Twelve effects work on color or sharpness: Blur, Brightness Decrease, Brightness Increase, Film Grain, Gray Scale, Hue–Cycles Entire Color Spectrum, Pixelate, Posterize, Sepia Tone, Smudge Stick, Threshold, and Water Color. You can get an idea of what these do by the name; make sure to try them out on a clip to get a good handle on how they look.

Four effects apply transition-type effects from or to a solid black or white image: Fade In, From Black; Fade Out, To Black; Fade In, From White; and Fade Out, To White.

> The fade effects are pretty good, but you might want greater control over the duration and look of these transitions. Another way to perform a fade on a clip is to use a solid color still image between clips and then apply a fade transition between them.
>
> TIP

The last three effects—Old, Older, or Oldest—make the movie look old in varying degrees, hearkening back to days of scratchy newsreel footage or the silent film era. These are great for adding a nostalgic look to your movie.

ADDING OR REMOVING VIDEO EFFECTS

To add a video effect to a clip, use these methods:

- If you're in the Storyboard view, drag an effect from the Video Effects collection and drop it onto the clip.

- If you're in the Timeline view, drag an effect from the Video Effects collection and drop it directly onto the clip.

See that gray star in the lower-left corner of the clip in the storyboard? It changes to a blue star when you add the first effect. When you add a second effect to the same clip, the star picks up a shadow, indicating that there are multiple effects on the clip. Figure 2-5 shows an example of what a clip looks like with multiple effects on it. In the timeline, the clip starts without a little gray star but picks up the blue one when you add an effect. A second blue star appears behind the first to show when you've added multiple effects to the clip.

TESTING AND FINE-TUNING YOUR EFFECTS

As with transitions, you'll want to play back the effects you apply to a clip to see how they look. To play back the clip with its effects, you can use these methods:

- If you're in the Storyboard view, click the clip with the effects and then click the Play Storyboard button or the Play button on the Monitor pane.

- If you're in the Timeline view, click the Time track or slide the playback bar to the beginning of the clip. Then click the Play Timeline button or the Play button on the Monitor pane.

Figure 2-5
This video clip has several effects.

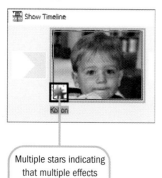

Multiple stars indicating that multiple effects have been applied

Your clip plays in the Monitor pane, showing you what the effects look like. If you need to get a clearer picture of the effects, you can click the Full Screen button or press Alt+Enter.

You can use as many as six effects on each clip. They can be the same one six times, or they can be six different ones. Any combination of up to six will work, but some might cancel each other out. Some of the easiest ones to visualize canceling are the clip rotation effects. For example, rotating a clip 90 degrees and applying the effect four times would end up with it rotated a full 360 degrees, turning it totally around and back to where it started. If you forget which effects you've applied, hover your mouse over the star in the Storyboard view to see a ToolTip that lists the currently applied effects. You can do the same in the Timeline view although Movie Maker can get a little picky about where your mouse hovers and what information it will display.

While you work with effects, you'll find that it not only matters which effects you've applied to a clip but in which order you've applied them. To change the effect order, you need to work with the Add Or Remove Video Effects dialog box. It lists the available effects in Movie Maker and lets you change the effect order and add or remove effects without dragging and dropping.

To open the Add Or Remove Video Effects dialog box, follow these steps:

1. Right-click a clip in either the storyboard or timeline.

2. Click Video Effects.

Figure 2-6 shows the dialog box that appears. You can also open the dialog box by clicking Clip, Video, and then Video Effects. Movie Maker will apply the effects in the sequence they're listed in the right column. If you want to move an effect up or down the list, click any of the displayed effects in the right column and then click the Move Up or Move Down button.

To add a video effect, highlight one in the Available Effects column and click the Add button. This adds the effect at the top of the list. To remove an effect, click an effect in the Displayed Effects list and then click Remove. When you're done changing the effect order, or adding or removing effects, click OK.

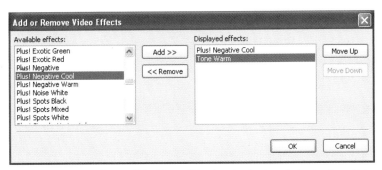

Figure 2-6 The Add or Remove Video Effects dialog box, showing two effects already applied to a clip

If you want to delete all the effects on a clip, select the star in the Storyboard view and then press Delete. That's much easier than opening the dialog box for effects and removing them individually.

You can get a lot of neat results by applying a number of effects to the same video clip, or you can get some pretty ugly-looking ones. You can spend a lot of time playing with them to see what works—and what doesn't. It's a good time to experiment with different combinations of video effects to see how they look on your clip.

TIP
You can add two commonly used video effects—Fade In, From Black and Fade Out, To Black—to a clip without having to go into the collection to get them. All you need to do is highlight and right-click a clip in the project and select Fade In or Fade Out.

Working with Video Transitions, Effects, and Still Pictures

You can use the same transitions and effects for still pictures or for changing from a still picture to a video clip. All the information about using effects on video clips also applies to still pictures, perhaps with a couple exceptions. For example, the default duration setting of five seconds is pretty good for general use. On the other hand, if you have a lot of still images that'll use something other than a five-second duration, it's a good idea to change the duration setting before you add them to the timeline. Once in the timeline, you can only change the image duration individually, using the trim handles. You can change picture duration by clicking Tools | Options, and then selecting the Advanced tab; then set any interval from one-eighth of a second to 30 seconds. Otherwise, you might find yourself trying to change them individually, which can be repetitive and annoying if you have a lot of images to change.

You can also change the duration of the picture on the Video track by dragging the trim handles, much like you can with any other clips. Speaking of trim handles, you can pull the handles for a still image as far as you'd like to change the clip's duration. You can pull the rightmost handle to the left to make the image play for as little as one-eighth of a second, the minimum default setting for the option; there doesn't seem to be a maximum to which you can pull the trim handle. When the timeline is longer than six hours, a pop-up dialog box will warn you about the project being longer than six hours and it taking a long time for Movie Maker to save it as a movie.

You can experiment for hours and hours just by testing the various ways you can apply effects to still images. Try overlapping a couple of the same images and apply different effects to each to see how they can morph and flow into one another.

Adding Titles and Credits

You can add cool titles, credits, and other text just about anywhere in your movie. You might be tempted to think of titles and credits as separate from text effects, but they're really the same. In Movie Maker, there really isn't any reason to distinguish between the use of text based on where it appears. You can use text as an introductory item before the movie, as credits at the end, or on top of or between clips in the timeline. Text is really easy, lots of fun, and can be truly amazing. In Figure 2-7, you see that you can place text anywhere in the movie.

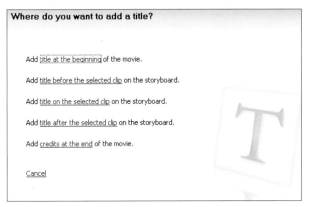

Where do you want to add a title?

Add title at the beginning of the movie.

Add title before the selected clip on the storyboard.

Add title on the selected clip on the storyboard.

Add title after the selected clip on the storyboard.

Add credits at the end of the movie.

Cancel

Figure 2-7
You can create text anywhere in your movie using this screen as the starting point.

In the previous chapter, you added text to your first movie when you built opening credits. In this section, you'll learn how to add text at any point in a movie and easily move it someplace else. For example, if you move the text to the Title Overlay track in the timeline, the text will assume a transparent background to show the underlying video. If you move it to the Video track, it'll turn into a video clip of text with a solid background color.

> Text isn't stored in the Movie Maker collection database; instead, it's specific to your project.
>
> NOTE

CREATING AND PLAYING A TITLE OR CREDIT

There are two ways to add text to the timeline. To create new text, follow these steps:

1. Switch to the Timeline view.

2. Click Tools | Titles And Credits. Alternatively, you can click the Tasks button to show the Movie Tasks pane, and then click Edit Movie | Make Titles Or Credits. Both methods will bring you to the same screen shown in Figure 2-7.

3. Click one of the links depending on where you want your text effect to appear.

4. Type text into either or both of the text areas. The top box displays larger text than the lower box.

5. Your text will play through twice on the monitor.

6. Click Done, and add a title to the movie.

7. Use the various Play controls to preview your text.

Your text appears in the timeline in the place you selected, such as in the Video track or in the Title Overlay track. Hover your mouse over the text, either on the Video track or on the Title Overlay track, and you can see the text you entered as well as the text's duration. Grab the text and move it to the left or right in the timeline to change where it starts and stops. The text clip also has trim handles, and, just like still images, you can make the text duration as long or as short as you like. Figure 2-8 shows the timeline with text in the Title Overlay track.

Figure 2-8
Text added to the Title Overlay track

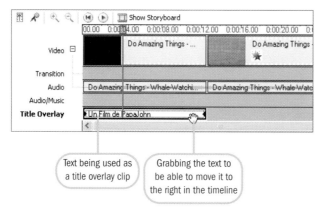

If you want, you can have two overlapping text clips on the Title Overlay track that apply to the same clip or clips on the Video track. Create two text clips, and you can move them, overlap them, and trim them on the Title Overlay track just as you would with any other clip.

ANIMATING YOUR TEXT

By default, when you first create text, Movie Maker 2 applies a fade in, pause, and fade out effect. Where do these come from? Movie Maker lets you change the animations applied to your text, so you don't have to stick with the default fade effect. You can use animations to make your text be crazy or classy, depending on the mood you're setting.

CHANGING TEXT ANIMATION

With your text in the timeline's Title Overlay track, double-click it to get back into the text dialog box. Click Change The Title Animation. A list appears that contains 25 animation options for one-line titles, nine for two-line titles, and another nine for credits. Although they're grouped into these categories, in reality you can use any of the animations for any of your text clips. To see what an animation does to your text, click the animation in the list and watch the preview in the Monitor pane. To apply any one of these animations to your text, select it and then click Done.

The amount of text you can use in a text clip will vary by the specific animation. Some animation effects change the text layout or give you specific fields to use (such as credits), so click Edit The Title Text to go back and see how much room you have to use. In most text clips you can press Enter to force a break to a new line; in others, the Tab key moves you from field to field faster than using your mouse. There's probably a limit to the amount of text you can use, but it's more likely that you or your audience will get bored reading all the text before you reach the limit.

CHANGING TEXT FONT AND COLOR

When you add text, the default text font and color are OK for most projects, but you might have a project that calls for more. Movie Maker 2 lets you change the text font, text color, text size, text placement, and text variations such as bold or italic text. There are a lot of options to choose from that you can use to enhance your text.

To change your text, double-click the text clip to get back into the text dialog box. Click Change The Text Font And Color. The Select Title Font And Color page appears, as shown in Figure 2-9, with the possible options for your text. The options are as follows:

Font This drop-down list shows you all the TrueType fonts installed on your computer. When you select one of the fonts in the list, the Monitor pane shows you what your text looks like using the selected font. The default is Microsoft Sans Serif.

Bold, Italics, Underline These buttons change your font's appearance. You can click any or all three of these to apply to your text.

Color These buttons let you change the font color and background color when the clip is on the Video track. Clicking either button opens the standard Windows color palette. Note that you can get creative and define custom colors to match your movie's design. The default font color is white; there's no background color by default when on the Title Overlay track, but the default is dark blue when on the Video track.

Transparency This slider changes the transparency percentage from 0 percent (or opaque so that no background shows through) to 90 percent (which makes your text very light).

Size These options increase or decrease the text size. No point size is shown, just smaller and larger buttons. Notch it up and down, and watch the Monitor pane to preview what the change in size is doing. It's a highly interactive experience.

Position These buttons let you position your text to be left-justified, centered, or right-justified. The default is centered.

Change any, all, or none of the settings, and then watch the changes in the monitor. Once you're satisfied, click Done. Your new settings are applied to your text and will play at the appropriate place in your timeline. If you want to use the same text settings with different text, it's simple to copy your text clip. In the Timeline view, click and drag the clip. While you drag, press Ctrl; then simultaneously release it and the mouse button elsewhere on the Video track. This makes a copy of your clip on the Video track. You can use this copying technique for any clip in the timeline or even for copying between the Video and Title Overlay tracks.

Figure 2-9 The Select Title Font And Color page has all the settings you need to enhance your text.

Here's a neat text effect to play with: create text for a film clip but don't add text yet. Apply the Scroll, Inverted one-line animation, and then change the text to the Wingding2 font using bold and italic effects. Change to black text, set to 0 percent transparency, and set the text to a large but not the largest text size, and center it. Type a string of the following letters: t u v w x y z. Watch the preview in the Monitor pane. With a little tweaking, you can turn this into a countdown effect. And, when you're done with the Wingding font, try Webdings!

APPLYING VIDEO EFFECTS TO A TEXT CLIP

If you place a text effect on the Video track (or in the storyboard), you can apply video effects to it. This lets you experiment with rotating your text, fading your text in or out, and cycling the background hue.

When you first place text on the Video track, your effect has white text on a blue background, instead of the white text with a transparent background it had when it was on the Title Overlay track. Switch to the Storyboard view and add a couple video effects to the text clip using the method discussed earlier in the chapter. Preview your project. You'll see that effects work on text just as they do on video clips or still pictures, and you can stack, rearrange, or delete them as with any other video clip.

Making AutoMovies

Sometimes your creativity is resting, and other times you just want to have some fun without spending a lot of time on clips, transitions, and effects. Movie Maker 2 has a neat feature that will help you in both circumstances. And who knows, it might just spark an idea for a project or turn into one. An AutoMovie is just that, one that Movie Maker makes for you. It'll take care of the editing, and it's really easy to do. Follow these steps:

1. Start with a new project timeline with nothing on it.

2. Select a collection that has a bunch of videos, still images, and a music clip. The duration of the music has to be at least 30 seconds. If you already have a collection full of video you'd like to use as an AutoMovie test subject, import or copy a music clip into the collection.

3. Select the collection.

4. Click Tools | AutoMovie.

5. Select one of the five AutoMovie editing styles (as shown in Figure 2-10):

   Flip and Slide   Flip, slide, reveal, and page curl video transitions are applied between your clips.

   Highlights Movie   This creates a clean and simple movie with simple cuts, fades, a basic title, and credits.

Music Video This uses quick edits for fast beats and longer edits for slow beats. Kids with short attention spans will love this option.

Old Movie Video effects are applied to clips to make an older-looking movie, such as a newsreel or silent movie.

Sports Highlights This creates a movie with fast pans and zooms to capture the action and adds an exploding title and credits to the beginning and end.

6 If you want to add a title, click Enter A Title For The Movie. Type the title in the text area.

7 If you want to add music, click Select Audio Or Background Music. You can browse for a particular music clip to add and then adjust volume levels.

8 Click Done to edit the movie.

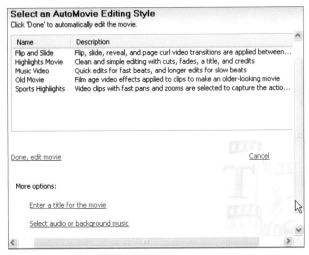

Figure 2-10 The Select An AutoMovie Editing Style page shows you the quick movie styles you can create from your collection of clips, still images, and audio.

Movie Maker will analyze the files and music and fill the timeline with video and still image clips, transitions, music, and a title. Preview the project to see how Auto-Movie used your clips. Relax, and enjoy it; if you like it enough, save it as a project and improve it from there.

TIME-LAPSE PHOTOGRAPHY MADE EASY

Movie Maker 2 gives you the power to create time-lapse photography without investing in expensive equipment, timers, or other hardware. Time-lapse photography uses either a still camera or a movie camera to take one picture at regular intervals—for example, once a minute, once every 15 minutes, once an hour, or once a day. With a digital studio, though, you can create these amazing effects without requiring the hardware or a full editing studio. By using a combination of still images, transitions, and effects, you can create a movie that looks like it was shot by a true time-lapse setup and then massaged in a real darkroom.

One way you can build time-lapse movies is to take pictures from a clip once every certain number of frames, such as once every five frames. Drag and drop these frames onto the storyboard. You might need to experiment with this to see how smoothly you want the "time lapse" to flow. Something that changes slowly, such as the view out your window from a Web cam, is more amenable to time-lapse treatment than the same Web cam focusing on a freeway's traffic flow.

Another way, and a fun way, is to use a single image repeatedly but change the types of transitions and video effects you apply between each instance of the image. You could create a hyperkinetic video with a shot of a single flower going through all kinds of transitions and changes over a short time period.

Think of other ways to adjust time by playing with single images or single frames as clips in the timeline. The options are almost endless.

The AutoMovie feature will use your selected music file and make the movie based on its duration. It's limited to a single music file. If you opt for the Music Video style, the music will be used and the audio on the video clips will be muted.

You could also make an AutoMovie without a music file, using video clips that have audio tracks. If you don't use a music file, AutoMovie will limit the duration of the movie to a maximum of three minutes, plus some extra time for titles. The video portion of such a movie might be interesting, but the stacked-up audio clips might play back disjointedly. Don't select the Music Video option for such a movie—the audio of the clips would be muted, and you wouldn't have the music file. Use one of the other four styles to hear the audio of the clips.

Learning More About Importing Video and Still Images

Most of this chapter has focused on creating transitions and effects for your movie to bring it up to "amazing" level. As you've probably discovered, you can go a long way and create a lot of features with the tools and techniques you've learned so far. But all techniques being equal, nothing beats starting with great footage and quality images. If your source material is high quality, your movie will turn out that much better, and your friends will be astonished at the work you're able to create on your own computer.

In Chapter 1, you saw how to capture footage from a camcorder. At the time, several options weren't explored. Now is the time for you to learn about those options and how they can improve your movie-making skills.

SETTING VIDEO CAPTURE OPTIONS

The options in the Video Capture Wizard will vary a bit with the capabilities of your computer and the devices being used for capturing. Movie Maker will check your computer and capturing devices and only offer you choices in the wizard that will work for you. For example, if you don't have a video capture device that works with your computer, you'll get an error message that says, "A video capture device was not detected. Verify that a device is turned on and connected properly, and then try again." It's information such as this that can prevent a lot of frustration later when it's time to build your movie. Three pages in particular within the Video Capture Wizard are worth some study: the Video Setting page, the Capture Method page, and the Capture Video page.

USING THE VIDEO SETTING PAGE

On the Video Setting page, shown in Figure 2-11, you're faced with a quality vs. file size decision. Although the first choice of Best Quality For Playback On My Computer (Recommended) is always recommended by Movie Maker, you should make a selection based on the playback capabilities of your audience's computers and other playback hardware, not your personal computer. At the bottom half of the page are two areas with information about the video capture settings: the Setting Details area and the Video File Size area. While you choose different capture options, these settings will change to show you the capture rates as well as the potential amount of file space that will be consumed.

If you're making CDs or DVDs for your audience, then the second choice of Digital Device Format (DV-AVI) is more appropriate. This file format will contain the greatest amount of data and information for your use, which means the final movie quality will be higher. The trade-off is in hard disk space. This format will use approximately 12 gigabytes of hard disk space per hour of captured video from your camcorder. You can see that even a medium-size project, with only a few hours of raw footage, will rapidly fill most hard disks at this setting. Serious video hobbyists and professionals will have

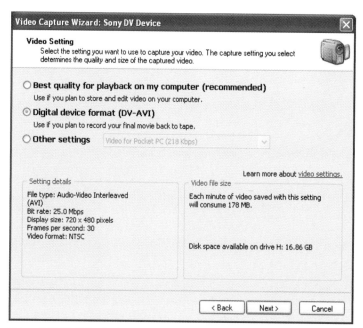

Figure 2-11 The Video Setting page shows you how much hard disk space will be needed for each minute of footage.

large amounts of hard disk storage for projects for just this reason. For more information on beefing up your computer for industrial-strength video handling, see Chapter 7.

The Other Settings drop-down menu will list a variety of playback devices you might use. If you know you'll play your movie on one of these devices and the quality will be acceptable, select the device here. However, any choice other than DV-AVI will use video compression to reduce the original camcorder footage to a smaller file, and your finished movie will be compressed again by Movie Maker 2 when you save it. Each compression step results in some reduction in video quality, which you'll notice if you try to play the finished movie back on another device.

USING THE CAPTURE METHOD PAGE

The next page is the Capture Method, as shown in Figure 2-12. It offers you the choice of automatically capturing the whole tape, which is typically one hour for a digital video camcorder, or of manually taking the controls to select the sections of the tape you want. The Show Preview During Capture check box at the bottom of the screen cautions you that previewing during the capture session possibly affects the quality of the captured file.

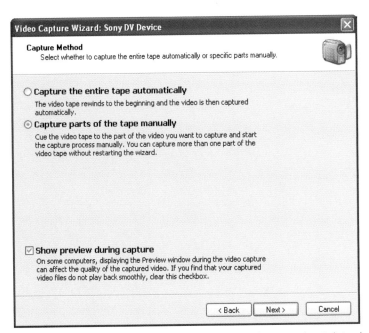

Figure 2-12 The Capture Method page lets you select automatic or manual capturing and gives you the ability to view your capture while it occurs.

USING THE CAPTURE VIDEO PAGE

On the next page of the wizard, shown in Figure 2-13, you can view what's on the camcorder and select the video segments you want to capture. Some camcorders support the computer being able to control the camcorder's playback VCR functions. For those that don't, you'll have to start and stop using the camcorder itself. If your camcorder does support it, it's nice to just turn on the camcorder, set it aside, and then control the capture from within the wizard.

Use the VCR-type controls under the wizard's monitor to get the tape to where you want to start a capture. Then back up a few seconds before the beginning of the clip to get a running head start, and click the Start Capture button. A few extra seconds often comes in handy during editing and gives you room to easily adjust the trim points. The wizard's monitor shows you the capture in progress, and you can listen to it on your camcorder's speaker during the capture session.

Start and stop the capture as you want. The data on the wizard's screen will tell you how much hard disk space has been used so far and how much is left on the drive you're creating the new file on. Movie Maker 2 will create clips when the wizard finishes while it imports the source file into your collection if you select that option.

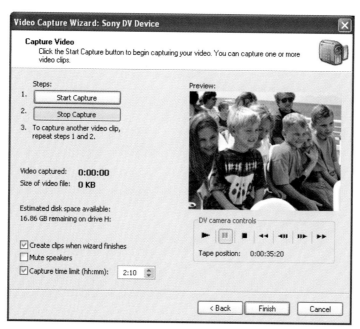

Figure 2-13 The Capture Video page is ready to capture a clip from the camcorder's raw footage.

When you've finished your capturing, click the Finish button and the wizard will copy its temporary capture file to the final one in your chosen folder, using the filename you selected earlier.

PERFORMING AUTOMATIC CLIP SPLITTING

Movie Maker provides an option for automatic clip creation during the video importing process. Figure 2-14 shows the Import File dialog box and the Create Clips For Video Files check box to turn on and off the automatic clip splitting feature.

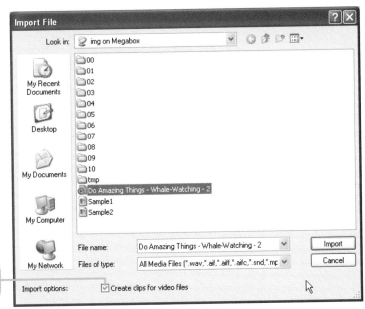

Option to automatically create clips during the import

Figure 2-14 The Create Clips For Video Files option can quickly generate clips from a video source file.

CREATING A "SILENT MOVIE"

This chapter focuses on the editing environment and using visual effects in your movies that will amaze your family and friends. Now, what better way to show off those editing and visual effects skills than by making a silent movie—where visual effects are what it's all about?

You can put your movie together using the following tools:

Video footage   It doesn't have to be fancy footage, but the sillier, the better. If you really want to have fun, have your kids dress in adult clothing and goof off around the house for a while, with you filming them while they go.

Video effects   The biggies here are a combination of Grayscale and any of the "film age" effects. Try experimenting with multiple instances and combinations of these to see which delivers the best "silent movie" experience without blurring parts so much that you can no longer pick out detail. Once you find a combination you like, you can use the Storyboard view to copy and paste the effects from the first clip to the others.

Text clips   Create a generic text clip that you can copy elsewhere in your movie. A good starter text clip uses bold Palatino Linotype, black background, white lettering, no transparency, a text size small enough to fit the screen, centered text, and a Basic Title (text appears with no motion or fade) animation. You can apply the same video effects to the text clip to keep the look consistent.

Audio   In the old days, silent movies weren't truly silent. There was the ratcheting sound of the projector showing the film, or in the bigger theaters there was a piano player who played a "soundtrack" to go with the film. Chapter 3 covers audio; if you want to add these sound effects to your film, read that chapter to learn how to work with audio and then come back here to finish the project. In the meantime, you can mute any audio tracks that accompany your video footage by following these steps:

1 Switch to the Timeline view.

2 Select the audio clip in the Audio track you want to mute.

3 Click Clip | Audio | Mute. This will mute the video's Audio track.

Now you can get creative! One of the best parts of this project is that you can pick out the *worst* clips you filmed and turn them into hilarious footage. Put words in people's mouths by using some creative text on the title clips. You can weave anything into your silent movie—if you dare! To get you inspired, the graphic below gives you a glimpse into the beginning of a really new old movie.

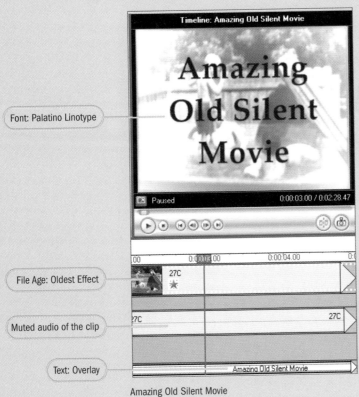

Amazing Old Silent Movie

If your source file was created by a digital camcorder, or the source file is a DV-AVI one, Movie Maker will look at the time code data embedded in the file and make a new clip each time you stopped and restarted the camcorder. If your source file is an analog one, Movie Maker uses scene detection methods to create the clips, sensing the different light levels that occur when a scene changes.

Although automatic clip creation can be a quick option to get you started with raw footage, you'll probably prefer to manually split clips after you get more experience working with Movie Maker. You'll have a better sense of the footage you've filmed, and you'll know the clips better while you go through them.

SETTING VIDEO CLIP PROPERTIES

After a while, when you start mixing and matching clips between collections and into projects, you might lose track of where the clip came from and what its properties are. Fortunately, Movie Maker keeps track for you. Right-click a clip, and then click Properties. The available information includes the following:

- Thumbnail image (using the first frame of the clip).

- Clip name.

- Duration, start time, and stop time.

- Source file type, location, bit rate, and file size. If the location is longer than the window that shows the clip information, linger over it with your mouse and a ToolTip will pop up with the full path and filename.

- Video pixel width, height, bit rate, and frame rate.

- Audio bit rate, number of channels, sample rate, and sample size.

This is extremely helpful if you want to find out whether the clip's resolution will work well with your latest project.

Making Your Workspace Match Your Style

You can modify the Movie Maker workspace to match the way you work, and it also has a bunch of shortcuts that can save you time from "mousing around."

Grab the horizontal divider in the main Movie Maker 2 window with your mouse. Move it up and down to see how the position affects what you see. Moving it upward makes the storyboard space bigger so you see each thumbnail better, but you only see about four or five clips at a time. Moving it back down lets you see a dozen or more of the clips but with smaller thumbnails. Figure 2-15 shows the storyboard with the divider moved down to see the greatest number of thumbnails at once.

Figure 2-15 Moving the window divider down maximizes the number of clips on the storyboard.

Figure 2-16 shows the divider moved upward as high as it can go, maximizing the timeline.

Now switch to the Timeline view. Click the plus and minus zoom buttons located just above the timeline, and you can zoom in or out from the timeline anywhere from seven seconds to two-and-a-half hours or more, depending on the resolution of your computer's monitor. The Page Up and Page Down keys also zoom you out and into the timeline, respectively; they work the same way as the zoom buttons but take less mouse work. The F9 key zooms the project to fit the timeline, saving you multiple clicks of the zoom buttons or presses of the Page Up and Page Down keys.

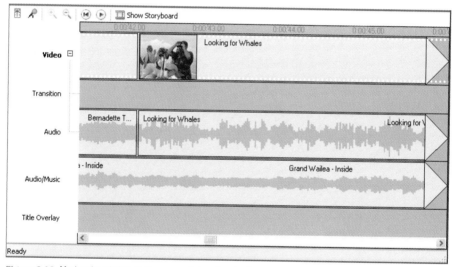

Figure 2-16 Moving the window divider up maximizes the timeline.

If you have a mouse wheel, scroll the wheel. This will result in the timeline scrolling left or right so you can quickly move back and forth along the tracks to the next edit point.

Highlight a clip in the timeline, and press Alt+Enter. You'll see the preview in full-screen mode. Use the key combination again to get back. If you forgot what keys you used to get to the full-screen mode, use the trusty old Esc key to get back to the normal project view.

BUFFING UP YOUR MOVIE

It's time to take a critical look at your first project you created in Chapter 1. In the creative environment of movie editing, you'll be the one who judges how good the project is, invites others for a preview, solicits feedback, determines what to do with that feedback, and knows when to call the work "finished."

STEP 1: DO A THOROUGH REVIEW

What's good but could be better while you move your project toward amazing? Some aspects to look for include the following:

Clip duration   Some clips are too long or too short; you'll know which ones they are while you watch your movie. Write notes to yourself about which clips need some fine-tuning. You might need to go back and recapture some video footage if you need to make a clip longer but don't have any extra frames available in your source file.

Image repetition   Sometimes repetition is good, and sometimes it's bad. If you keep seeing shots of one person or one building over and over in a sequence, or throughout your movie, maybe you need to mix up the images a bit more.

Clip tempo   Some clips are full of action, with events happening all over the place. Others are downright pastoral. Does your movie jump from one tempo to another in a jarring manner? Maybe you need some intermediate clips, some text effects, or some midtempo transitions.

Effects usage   Attention-diverting transitions or distracting video effects can really mess up an otherwise excellent movie. In nearly all cases, less is more. Find less distracting transitions and effects; go for class over crass.

"Filler" material   It's tempting to add as much usable footage and images as possible just to make sure you cover everything. If this happens, you'll need to revisit your theme or movie topic and either change your topic or be ruthless about which clips fit the best.

Text amount   You might know what all the scenes are about, but many of your viewers won't. Consider adding titles and credits between scenes to help clue in viewers as to what's going on.

STEP 2: MAKE THE GOOD STUFF BETTER

It's easy to fix the bad stuff. But the goal is to enhance the good stuff and make it amazing. Some guidelines to work with include the following:

Length   Don't pay attention to the movie's length while editing. Unless you have an actual time limit for your finished movie, such as for a contest or because of disk space, don't be constrained by a length factor.

Trimming   You'll spend a lot of time making small adjustments to trim points so your clips look just right. Zoom in on your clip so you can make small trim adjustments comfortably with your mouse.

Transitions   Play with the overlap between clips and the transition duration. Learn where the transitions happen smoothly and where they look clunky. Between this and adjusting trim points, you'll spend most of your time working on these two actions.

Timing   Judicious use of effects can really make a clip pop out and say, "Wow!" Applying the Slow Down, Half video effect to the key moment in a movie (the winning basket, the tag at home plate, the unveiling of a new painting) both draws attention to the importance of the moment and gives viewers more time to enjoy the details without them flying by. Look for moments when you can put timing effects to good use. (Note that audio also plays at half speed. See Chapter 3 for information on working with audio clips so you can use the audio from the slowed-down clip at regular speed.)

STEP 3: IMPROVE OR DISCARD THE REST

Go through your list of items to work on from step 1, and see which items you can fix and which are easier to leave on the cutting-room floor. Some fixes are easy, and others might take some experimenting to see if you can move them into the "good" category. Try not to get distracted if you're working on one problem and see another that needs a quick fix; by the time you get back to the original problem, your creative flow is redirected and it's difficult to get it back into the original thought process.

STEP 4: SAVE THE MOVIE, REVIEW IT, AND DO IT AGAIN

You can keep previewing and tweaking it until you either get tired of it or your production deadline arrives. If you're doing this purely for your own enjoyment, you can keep working on it until your next good idea for a project takes over and you move onto new footage and new ideas.

Glossary

cross-fade
A method of smoothly moving from one video clip or photo to another. With a cross-fade transition, the frames in the playing clip fade out while the frames in the new clip fade in. In the film industry, the same process is called a "dissolve."

duration
The length of time that clips or still images play in a movie.

DV-AVI
The acronym for "Digital Video–Audio Video Interleave." It's a Microsoft audio/video format that encodes camcorder data in a suitable format for use in Movie Maker and other video editing programs.

fade
A transition that dissolves from the frames in one clip to the frames in the following clip. It's also used to fade out (fade to black) or fade in (fade from black into the clip).

simple cut
When the last frame of one clip is followed directly by the frame of another clip.

- **Creatively Use Audio, Music, and Narration**
- **Import Music into Your Collections**
- **Add Sound That Enhances Your Video**
- **Adjust Clip Volume and Add Professional-style Audio Transitions**
- **Complement Your Movie with Narration**

Enhancing the Soundscape

CHAPTER 3

Dialogue. Sound tracks. Sound effects.
Background noise. All these are crucial
parts of a movie, and without them your
movie would seem like it was missing
something. Watch one of your clips without sound, or watch your favorite movie
on TV with the sound off. It's amazing
how much less of a movie it seems
without sound. Sound is key not only for
dialogue, but when you add music and
sound effects, you create and enhance
the mood. Who can forget the deep,
four-note "ba-dum, ba-dum" sounds in
the movie *Jaws* that announced something deadly was lurking in the deep?
Without those notes, the scene would've
just been nice scenes of people swim-
ming. Well, maybe not exactly *nice*, but
you get the idea.

Spectacular pyrotechnics aren't needed with audio, just straightforward fades and overlapping cuts.

Coming Attractions

Sound can make or break your movie, but it doesn't have to be in-your-face obvious. Moviegoers rarely notice music sound tracks, but they'd notice if a sound track wasn't present. Sound tracks are usually theme appropriate, subtle, and powerful. Fortunately, you don't need to put yourself under that kind of pressure; you're not betting millions of dollars on whether your movie will make or break at the box office!

This chapter introduces you to the joys of adding audio to your movie and making your project even more amazing by creatively using audio. You'll learn to import various clips, music, or even sound effects; you'll learn how to add them to the timeline and perform basic transitions; you'll learn how to make more complex audio tracks; and you'll learn how to record and use narration for your own voice-over work in your movie. Let's get started.

Designing Your Movie's Audio

Some people are intimidated by the idea of manipulating the audio of a project. They get a mental picture of a recording studio, with bank after bank of knobs, dials, slides, and wires running everywhere. Fortunately, Movie Maker 2 gives you several easy-to-master techniques and effects that cover 99 percent of the audio effects you hear in any professional movie. Using them is as easy as building a movie by dragging and dropping: a few clips here and a few edits there, and soon you have a complete, professional-sounding audio track.

But just because the mechanics of building an audio track are easy doesn't mean you should leave it until the last minute. Don't put more than 90 percent of your editing time into making a really great movie and then quickly throw in some random music as background. The particular music, how loudly it plays relative to the video's accompanying audio track, and the music's tempo relative to the video clips all form the viewer's total experience. Spend some time thinking about the theme or topic for your movie, the kind of pacing you'll be using, and come up with ideas of music or sound tracks you think would match your overall story goals.

As you go through your movie and edit video clips, resist the temptation to keep realigning the audio with the video. Leave the music and audio editing until the end of your editing sessions. Don't try to align an exact beat in a song with an exact spot in a video clip while you're still tweaking the video. While you edit and fine-tune your movie, the position of each video clip in the timeline will be constantly changing. Even if you think the sequence of still images and video clips is perfect, editing the transitions will automatically cause further changes in the overall duration. For example, adding a two-second overlap for a transition will shave two seconds off the overall time, which in turn throws off your audio by two seconds. Save yourself the extra work and frustration, and leave the audio edits to the end.

Adding Music and Audio Clips to a Collection

One of the great aspects of enhancing the audio is that you aren't limited to what you captured on your video camera. You can use sound from just about anywhere: other film clips, music CDs, sound effect CDs, or anything you can convert into an audio file on your computer.

Movie Maker can use audio from any captured video source, and it can use music files from CDs if they've been ripped and saved in either MP3 or WMA format. You can use Windows Media Player on your computer to rip and save tracks to your computer in WMA format, and you can download music files in MP3 format from various audio-file services for use in Movie Maker.

> This book's introduction cautions you about using audio and video material that's under copyright protection. Be sure to read it first if you're using material that isn't your original work.
>
> NOTE

If you have audio files on your computer that aren't in the commonly used MP3, WMA, or WAV format, or another format that Movie Maker accepts, you'll need to convert them. See the book's Web site *http://www.papajohn.org* for information about conversion. Importing music files is even easier than importing video or capturing raw video footage:

1. Create a new collection for your audio files or select an existing collection to receive your new music clips.

2. Click File | Import Into Collections.

3. Browse to the folder where you keep your music files.

4. Select one or more music files you want to add to your collection.

5. Click Import. The files will be added to your selected collection.

Music clips in a collection all have the same thumbnail, a musical note. See Figure 3-1 for an example. If you change to the Details view, you'll see perhaps the most important property of each—the duration—which appears after the filename. (You can click View | Details, or you can click the Views button and then click Details to switch views.) If you want a three-and-a-half-minute music track for a movie, this is the view to use because it can sort by duration. See Figure 3-2 to see the music clips sorted by duration.

TIP You can also use My Computer to drag audio/music clips from any folder on your hard disk, and drop it into a selected collection's Contents pane.

Figure 3-1 Imported audio clips all show the same thumbnail in a collection.

Figure 3-2 Sort your audio files by duration if you need to find one with a specific time.

USE YOUR CAMCORDER AS A SOUND RECORDER

Don't just think of your camcorder as a tool to take video. The sound systems of today's digital camcorders record in CD-quality stereo sound. But many people don't always think of it as an easy-to-use substitute for a sound tape recorder or as an easy method of getting the sound into the computer and your project. A couple of examples illustrate how easy it is to capture sounds for use in your movies:

- In Chicago a few weeks ago, just when I started walking under a fairly long highway overpass, I started to hear the sounds of fire engines, police cars, and emergency vehicles above me. I whipped out my camcorder and started "shooting" at anything I heard, aiming at the sounds while they reverberated off the tunnel walls. I didn't even have to take the lens cap off to get a couple minutes of such great sound—the kind you can only get in a big city and when totally unprepared.

- Arriving home one night, I found the answering machine beeping as usual. One message was an excited granddaughter telling me about her first unassisted ride on her two-wheel bicycle, without training wheels. Before erasing the message, I put the camcorder up close to the answering machine and taped it. Later I got a copy of the camcorder scene that my son-in-law had taken of the event. I now have the two related but separate pieces for a movie project.

Getting the sound from the camcorder into your movie project is easy. It goes in the same way that the video goes in. Capture it, import it, and put the clip on the Audio/Music track in Movie Maker 2. You can use it with any of the video clips you're using.

Adding and Editing Audio Clips

When you want to work on your audio, switch to the Timeline view. As you've probably noticed, the Storyboard view is really only meant for working with video. If you try to drag a music or audio clip to the storyboard, Movie Maker will give you a friendly notice that you can add audio only to the timeline. It'll then switch to the Timeline view and add your audio clip there for you.

In the timeline, there are two places for your audio. The first is the Audio track that's part of the Video group of tracks. If you don't see the Audio track, click the plus sign next to the Video track to expand it and show the Audio track. The second place is on the Audio/Music track, which is immediately below the Audio track. The key difference between these two tracks is that the Audio track is for audio that's part of a video clip. When you capture video from a camcorder, you capture two different data streams: the video, which is encoded with video-specific information, and the audio, which is encoded with audio-specific information. These two data streams are parallel to but separate from each other—a feature that'll come in handy in a few moments.

To add audio to your movie, use one of these methods:

- If you're adding a music or sound effect clip, drag it from a collection and drop it onto the Audio/Music track.

- If you want to use both the audio and video portions of a video clip, drag the video clip from a collection and drop it onto the Video track, and the audio portion will automatically be included in the Audio track.

- If you want to use just the audio portion of a video clip, drag the video clip from a collection and drop it onto the Audio/Music track, and you can use the audio portion in the same way you use a music clip.

Figure 3-3 shows both a music clip and the audio portion of a video clip added to the timeline.

Unlike video or image clips that "snap" together to close gaps in the Video track, audio clips in the Audio/Music track can be moved anywhere and will stay where you move them.

If you want to delete a track from the timeline, use the same method as for video clips. Click the clip, and press Delete. Alternately, you can right-click the clip and then click Delete. Both methods will remove the clip from the timeline.

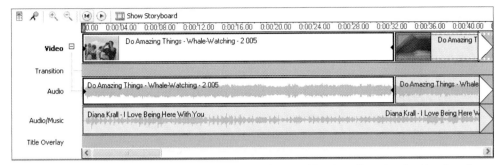

Figure 3-3 The Audio/Music track has a music clip on it, and the Audio track has the audio portion of a video clip on it.

SPLITTING AND COMBINING AUDIO CLIPS

You can split audio clips in the timeline using the same technique you used for video clips:

1. Slide the playback indicator to the point where you want to split the audio clip, or scroll through the timeline and then click the timeline to jump the playback indicator to that point.

2. Click the Split Clip button on the monitor, or click Clip | Split. You can also press Ctrl+L to split the clip.

Figure 3-4 shows an audio clip that has been split using this method. Notice the clip name remains the same for both halves.

You can also split a long music clip in the collection, just as you can with video clips. Move the seek bar to the appropriate time point on the monitor, and then split the clip. You might want to use this technique if there's a particular segment of a longer music piece that you'd like to use, especially if you might be using the original piece

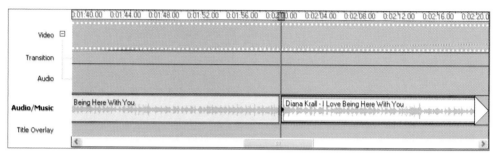

Figure 3-4 An audio clip has been split at the two-minute mark.

in a number of movies. Having the clip split appropriately is easier than repeatedly splitting it for each movie or repeatedly setting trim points for each movie. If you use this technique, make a copy of the clip in the collection and then work on the copy. That way, if you need to start over, you don't need to reimport the audio file and begin the process again.

You can combine audio clips the same way as video clips; the segments must have been contiguous in the original clip. You can't combine segments from different parts of a clip or from different audio clips.

To combine audio clips, select the clips you want to combine, right-click, and then select Combine. The clips are rejoined into one longer clip.

TRIMMING AUDIO CLIPS

Audio clips behave just like video clips in the timeline, with the same type of trim handles that video clips have. They work the same way, with any trimmed parts of the clip showing as gray areas in the timeline.

Sometimes it can be tricky to set the trim point exactly. Rather than playing the clip and trying to hit Pause at the point where you want to trim it, you can use the audiograph on the Audio track to help you set the trim points. To do this, follow these steps:

1. Use the monitor buttons or the Play Timeline and Pause Timeline buttons to preview the Audio track. Pause it relatively close to where you want to trim the audio tracks.

② Click and drag the divider bar upward between the timeline and the middle three panes.

③ Click the Zoom In button until you can't zoom in anymore.

This makes the Audio tracks as large as possible, and it lets you see the shape of the audio waves. Figure 3-5 shows the tracks enlarged and the timeline zoomed in to show the audio detail. This helps you determine where to trim the clip, which will typically be between audio peaks or at "quiet" points on the Audio track.

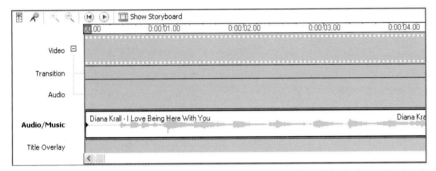

Figure 3-5 Maximize the timeline and zoom in all the way to see the audiograph details for precise trimming.

Adjusting the Audio Levels

Using some simple controls in Movie Maker, you can make audio adjustments for the audio levels, or volume, of audio and music clips and of the overall project.

ADJUSTING A SINGLE CLIP

To adjust the volume of an audio clip or the audio portion of a video clip, follow these steps:

① Right-click the clip.

② Click Volume. Figure 3-6 shows the Audio Clip Volume dialog box.

③ Move the slider to increase or decrease the clip's volume.

④ Click OK.

By default, a clip's volume is set to the middle of the slider scale. When you adjust the slider and click OK, the clip's audiograph changes to match the changes in volume. Test the volume by moving the playback bar to the start of the clip and clicking Play.

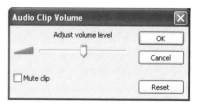

Figure 3-6 The Audio Clip Volume dialog box lets you adjust an individual clip's volume, reset to the defaults, or mute the audio.

If you need to return the volume to where it was in the beginning, click the Reset button on the dialog box to clear your adjustments.

Also, note that the dialog box has an option to mute the clip. You can mute a clip's audio here, or you can right-click the clip and select the Mute Clip command. When you mute a clip, the audiograph changes to a flat line.

BALANCING THE AUDIO AND AUDIO/MUSIC TRACKS

If you have multiple audio clips placed on both the Audio and Audio/Music tracks, you'll encounter situations where one track is louder than the other. When this happens, you can try to adjust each of the audio levels in each clip and hope to strike an acceptable balance, or you can use the Movie Maker Audio Levels dialog box to do it for you. Click the Set Audio Levels button in the timeline to open the Audio Levels dialog box.

Figure 3-7 shows the Audio Levels dialog box; it's a simple slider control that moves between the Audio From Video track and the Audio/Music track, and its default is midway between the two tracks. Move it in either direction, and preview the project to see what effect this has. The effect can vary depending on the clips in each track. To close the dialog box, you can either click the red × or click the Audio Levels button again.

The Audio Levels setting is global and applies to the *entire project*, not just the clips that happen to be selected when you open it. If you adjust the level, trying to compensate for extremes on two separate clips, you could throw the rest of the movie's levels out of balance. Depending on the project, you can think of the Audio From Video track as "foreground" and the Audio/Music track as "background" (or vice versa). If needed, set the balance between the two appropriately and then fine-tune any volume mismatches between clips by adjusting the audio levels for each clip.

Figure 3-7 You can adjust the balance between the two Audio tracks using the Audio Levels dialog box.

IT'S KARAOKE TIME!

A great project for working with audio is to create a karaoke version of a favorite song. A karaoke version consists of just an audio file and text clips with the lyrics on them. Naturally, when you get done with the karaoke version, there will be a little more to it than that.

Start with a favorite song from a music CD or movie, record it in either MP3 or WMA format, and then import it into a new collection. Windows Media Player can be especially helpful in locating and recording audio for your use. Next, if you don't know the lyrics by heart, use the Internet to search for the lyrics on the band's Web site or a fan's Web site. Save the Web page to your computer or copy and paste the lyrics into another program such as Notepad or WordPad.

Now add your music clip to the timeline, maximize the timeline, and zoom in as far as possible, as shown in the graphic below. Start with a title clip before the song actually starts, both to identify the song and artist and to give a few seconds of warm-up time for your budding vocal artists. Now build your text clips with the lyrics on them. Add them to the Video track, flashing the lyrics perhaps half a second to one second before they're actually sung in the music clip. You'll need to do some fiddling with the text clip duration to match them appropriately with the music.

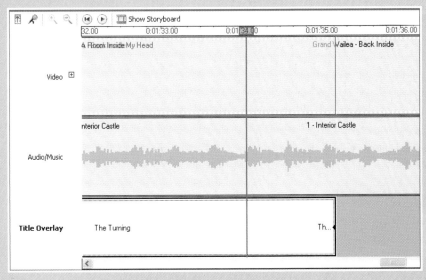

The timeline synchs up the lyrics with the music.

Next, you can add some video effects to the text clips. Don't make these too difficult or fancy because you want the karaoke singers to actually see the lyrics without straining. They don't have to be as static as cue cards, though, so create effects such as rotating the background color, having the lyrics fly in then fly out, and so forth. Add more fun and interest by mixing in your personal still and video clips, as shown in the graphic below.

Once you've worked your way through the entire song by building the text clips and editing them to fit the music, try performing the song yourself. If you crack yourself up trying to perform the song, chances are it'll be just as big a hit with your friends the next time you get together!

Now, let's have a little more fun. Sometimes, the song's lyrics are a bit muddled, and people hear some interesting variations on the song. For instance, Jimi Hendrix sang, "'Scuse me while I kiss the sky"; he *didn't* sing, "'Scuse me while I kiss this guy." But your friends might not know that. There are Web sites dedicated to misheard lyrics; swap a few of those lyrics into your karaoke version, and watch your friends' expressions as they expect to see the lyrics sung one way but see different words to sing instead. If you're really sneaky, you'll be filming this with your camcorder so you can get great footage for your *next* project.

You can add interesting still and video images to your text clips.

ADJUSTING THE WHOLE PROJECT

Once you know how to adjust individual clips and you can strike a balance between the different tracks in your project, you can use these methods to adjust all the audio clips in your project. Look at all the audiographs. You're looking for some consistency among the clips for how high the peaks are in each. The wave patterns give you good visual feedback about how the audio will play. Listen to the audio playback when you edit your movie, and see if there are any overly loud or quiet points that need adjustment. Use the audiographs to help you adjust the audio levels to achieve that consistency.

Adding Audio Transitions

Unlike video transitions, audio transitions are fairly simple. Spectacular pyrotechnics aren't needed with audio, just straightforward fades and overlapping cuts. After wrestling with video transitions and effects, and repeatedly fine-tuning and adjusting the effects, working with audio transitions is a breeze.

FADING IN OR FADING OUT ON AUDIO TRACKS

Similar to fading in or out on a video clip, you can fade the audio in or out. If your audio clip isn't overlapped by another clip, you can manually set a fade in or fade out transition for the clip. To set the fade, follow these steps:

1. Right-click the clip.

2. Click either Fade In or Fade Out from the menu.

You can also set a fade by clicking the clip, clicking Clip | Audio | Fade In or Fade Out. When you use this method, the fade's duration is less than a second.

> **NOTE**
>
> Any applied audio effect is maintained when you split an audio clip. If you've applied the Fade In effect and then split the clip, the effect is applied to both clips. If you combine two audio clips, any audio effects associated with the first clip are applied to the new combined clip, and the audio effects for the second clip are removed.

If you move two audio clips so they overlap each other on the same track, you automatically create a cross-fade, where the audio from one clip fades out and the other audio clip fades in. To overlap the clips, click and drag the clip on the right so it overlaps the clip on the left. A blue triangle appears that grows longer as the overlap increases. This indicates a fade between the two audio clips. Figure 3-8 shows a cross-fade in progress.

Use this cross-fade approach to achieve a long fade from or to silence. The default Movie Maker fade in and fade out occurs in less than a second. You can extend it to as long as you want by adding a *silent* audio clip and overlapping it with the audio clip that you want to fade. A silent audio clip is any audio clip of the length you want but with the sound muted. It's comparable to overlapping a video clip with a black still picture to achieve a long fade from or to blackness.

ADDING J-CUTS AND L-CUTS

Using audio transitions is easy and often adds a real touch of professionalism to your movies. Two transitions that automatically bump your movies up from good to amazing are the J-cut and the L-cut. These cuts are named for the look they have in the timeline. The audio can either start earlier than the associated video or linger for a bit after the video ends. If the audio starts earlier, it's referred to as a *J-cut*. If it continues afterward, it's called an *L-cut*. An example of each helps illustrate the concept.

You've seen J-cuts on nearly every cop show you've ever seen on TV. For example, the show comes back from a commercial, and you see the exterior of the station house. While you're looking at the exterior for several seconds, you hear office noises and two cops discussing the criminal they nabbed just before the commercial. The scene cuts to the station house interior, showing the two cops talking at a desk, and the rest of the show goes on from there. The second scene's audio starting during the first scene is a J-cut.

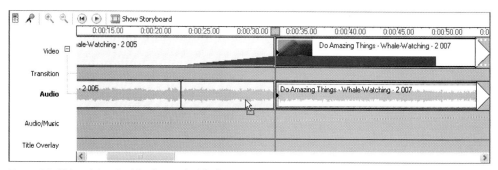

Figure 3-8 Click and drag the right clip over the left clip to create a cross-fade.

An L-cut works the other way. To use the same setting, the cops are in the station house discussing where to find a witness to the crime. While they get ready to put on their coats and leave, the video cuts to an exterior of an apartment house while the audio has them agreeing to go search for the witness near the apartment house. The first scene's audio continuing into the second scene is an L-cut.

The easier of the two is the L-cut. To make an L-cut, follow these steps:

1. Click and drag one video clip onto the Video track and then click and drag a second copy onto the Audio/Music track.

2. Do the same steps using the second video clip. You should now have two copies of each clip, one on the Video track and one on the Audio/Music track.

3. Click the first clip's Video track.

4. Click and drag the clip's trim handles to the left and trim the clip appropriately. When you release the handles, a gray overlap appears over the second clip in the timeline. Figure 3-9 shows what your cut should look like so far.

5. Click the second clip's Audio/Music track.

6. Click and drag the trim handles so the end of the clip matches the end of the video clip above it.

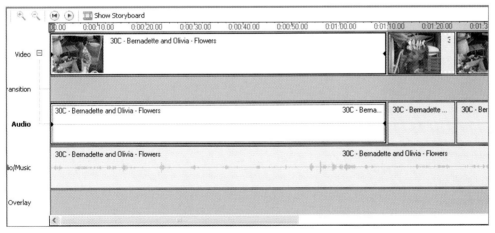

Figure 3-9 After you move the trim handles, the first clip's video overlaps the second clip.

7 Right-click the first video clip's matching Audio track, and click Mute.

8 Right-click the second video clip's matching Audio track, and click Mute.

9 Preview your cut.

The trickier of the two transitions is the J-cut, primarily because it involves more adjustment of trim points on video and audio clips than the L-cut. To make a J-cut, follow these steps:

1 Click and drag one video clip onto the Video track, and then click and drag a second copy onto the Audio/Music track.

2 Do the same steps using the second video clip. You should now have two copies of each clip, one on the Video track and one on the Audio/Music track.

3 Click the first clip's Audio/Music track.

4 Click and drag the trim handles to the left. A gap opens between the first and second clips in the Audio/Music track.

5 Click and drag the second clip's Audio/Music track to the left so that the two audio clips are adjacent again.

6 Click the second clip's Video track.

7 Click and drag the clip's trim point to the right. The gray overlap in the timeline should be at the same point as the two Audio/Music tracks. See Figure 3-10 for an example.

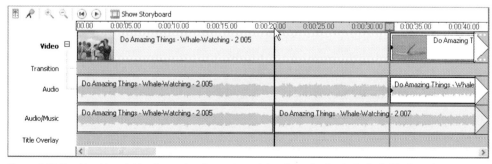

Figure 3-10 The video trim point has been set so the overlap matches the audio clips in the Audio/Music track.

8 If needed, click the second video clip and trim the stop point to match the Audio/Music track.

9 Right-click the first video clip's matching Audio track, and click Mute.

10 Right-click the second video clip's matching Audio track, and click Mute.

11 Preview your cut.

These cuts take a little bit of practice, but they're pretty easy once you've done a couple of them. By the time you've worked in a few fades, some sound effects, and some J-cuts and L-cuts, your movie's audio is already better than 99 percent of other home movies.

> Don't forget to use the "nudge" feature of Movie Maker 2 to move a selected clip to the left or right by a single frame. It comes in handy when synchronizing audio and video tracks.
>
> TIP

Adding Narration

Want to add a personal touch to your movies? You can add narrations to your audio track. Narrations are voice-overs you record that you add to an audio track as part of your movie's audio. Your narration can consist of nearly anything. You don't need a narration for every movie you make, but for some movies they're almost a requirement, such as a travelogue or running commentary on your family's vacation.

You can easily create a narration file within Movie Maker 2 by using the Narrate Timeline dialog box. To create a narration, you need a sound card with a microphone attached to it and working properly. Most audio cards ship with a microphone or microphone/headset combination; if you can't find one, check with your local computer store about ordering one for your system.

MAKE YOUR OWN MUSIC VIDEO

One of the easiest audio projects—and one of the most fun—is to create your own music video. Start with a favorite song from a music CD or movie, record it in either MP3 or WMA format, and then import it into a new collection. Windows Media Player can be especially helpful in locating and recording audio for your use. Don't try to be too ambitious and pick a 13-minute rock opera song; pick something that's quick, punchy, and won't drag on and bore your potential audience. Three minutes or so will do nicely.

You can start by adding your music clip onto the Audio/Music track before you add any other clips. Note the amount of time the clip takes up; you'll need to find or create that much video footage or combination of video and still images for your video. You can always finesse the audio by splitting or trimming the clip or fading in and out; for now, try to make the video match the audio instead of the other way around.

Next, start adding footage, still images, text effects, and whatever looks fun and fits with the music. You can apply video effects to slow down a video clip or speed it up, add sound effects in the Audio/Music track, and, in fact, do just about anything that adds fun and excitement to your video.

Once the footage is in place and edited, you can start playing with the audio. You can mute the original video's soundtrack and just have the music play, or you can have it softer but still audible beneath the music. Or you can have the music drop for a moment so you can clearly hear someone utter a not-very-polite phrase.

How can you adjust the volume to better hear that "not-very-polite" phrase? The volume of the entire clip changes when you use the clip's volume control. It's easy—just split the clip before and after the phrase, so you now have three clips in the timeline. Adjust the volume of the one that plays during the phrase, and leave the others alone. When the movie is rendered and played, the transition will be seamless.

Once you're satisfied, show your music video to your friends. Then hope they don't have a copy of Movie Maker and some camcorder footage of you sitting in their basement.

CREATING A NEW NARRATION

Creating a new narration in Movie Maker is easy; follow these steps:

1. Click the Narration icon in the timeline (the icon second from the left), or click Tools | Narrate Timeline. The Narrate Timeline dialog box appears.

2. Drag the playback indicator to an empty spot in the timeline.

3. Click Start Narration, and begin talking into the microphone.

4. When you're done with the narration, click Stop Narration.

When you're done with your narration, Movie Maker will create a new audio file, save it in your Narration folder, import it to the current collection, and place it in the time-line. The actual audio file is stored in the My Videos\Narration folder; the filename will start with the project name and end with a numbered suffix that increases auto-matically with each narration file.

You can set a number of options using the Narrate Timeline dialog box. Figure 3-11 shows the dialog box with Show More Options selected. The features and options are as follows:

Input Level   You can change the microphone's input level so that the narration isn't too loud or too soft. Speak into the microphone, and use the slider control to change the input level. The desired level is in the upper third of the meter without getting into the red area.

Limit Narration   This option limits the narration time to the free space in the timeline before the start of the next audio/music clip. If the narration isn't lim-ited, it'll continue until you stop it, even if other audio clips are in the timeline. The added narration will push the other audio/music clips out in the timeline. It's a good idea to use the Mute Speakers option while narrating, or existing audio will be playing at the same time the narration is being recorded. You'll usually want as clean a narration as possible and not the echo from other already recorded clips.

Narration Captured/Time Available   Movie Maker reports the amount of narra-tion captured so far and the remaining time available until the start of the next audio clip on the track. The remaining time will show only if you've selected the option to limit narration.

Audio Device This will default to the hardware device from which your audio comes. If you only have one audio capture device, it'll be the device listed. You probably won't need to change this setting.

Audio Input Source This will list six or seven choices, with the Microphone option being used for narration. Movie Maker will only work with those that are analog inputs. Again, you probably won't need to change this.

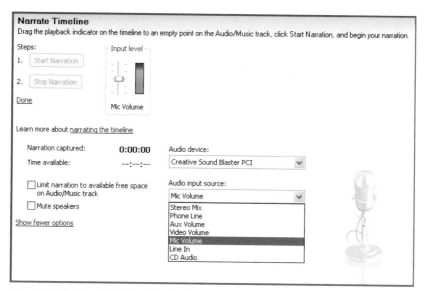

Figure 3-11 The Narrate Timeline dialog box lets you easily add narration.

USING NARRATION FILES

If you have other narration files from other projects, you can import and use them in the timeline the same way you use your music files or newly created narration files. If you have narration files in formats other than WMA, they'll also work. Just import them into a collection, and use them in your project. You can copy, split, delete, trim, mute, fade in, or fade out your narration clips just as you would any other clip.

Glossary

audio levels Generally the same as the volume.

audiograph The wave pattern shown in the Audio/Music track by an audio clip or the audio portion of a video clip.

J-cut An audio cut where the following scene's audio starts playing before the video.

L-cut An audio cut where the preceding scene's audio continues playing into the second scene's video.

narrations Voice-overs or other vocal clips you can add to an audio track.

rip The process of copying a file from one format to another. It is commonly used when referring to extracting video files from a CD or DVD, and doing whatever conversion is needed during it to get it from one place to another.

- **Set Up Your Standard Movie Options**
- **Organize Your Projects**
- **Build Your Video Resource Library**
- **Import Clips and Files**
- **Save and Back Up Your Files**

Preserving Your Movie Collection

CHAPTER 4

No good movie creator would dump film footage on the floor, have strips of it randomly hanging on coat hangers, or forget to put the source film and the edited film back into a film vault when the day's work is done. Yet many people take the same free-spirited, devil-may-care approach to caring for footage edited on computer. Not to sound like your mother, but you really ought to have neater habits in your virtual editing room.

Organization is something that's usually done long after it should've been started.

Coming Attractions

When you capture more raw footage and build more projects, the amount of information to keep track of multiplies. Wouldn't you like to know how to make your life easier and your editing smoother by learning a few key techniques? In this chapter, you'll look at the organizational side of movie making; along the way, you'll learn about keeping track of your footage using the finer points of video and audio conversion and backing up and saving your projects and files.

Setting Your Options

One of the first keys to organization is setting some general options that affect how your projects are built and how you work with them. By default, Movie Maker 2 ships with the options set up in a "one-size-fits-most" fashion. These settings will work for most people just starting out. However, by the time you've worked with Movie Maker a while, you'll want to change a few options to match more closely how you work or to configure your project for its eventual destination.

The first step is to open the Options dialog box and look at what's available. To do this, click Tools | Options. Two tabs are available for you to customize: the General tab and the Advanced tab. The first one to look at is the General tab, shown in Figure 4-1.

These options affect the overall behavior of Movie Maker regardless of which project you're working on. After you gain some experience, you'll want to change a few of these settings, especially if you add a second hard disk for movie-related storage. The options are as follows:

Default Author   The name you put here will appear in some media players when the movie is viewed. You can override this name for a particular project, or you can leave it blank (the default setting).

Temporary Storage   Movie Maker uses your hard disk to create and store temporary files while capturing video from your camcorder, while recording narrations, and while rendering movies. You can change this location if you run out of room on your C: drive or if you have a second hard disk with available space. See the Appendix for more information on working with specific hardware for Movie Maker 2.

Open Last Project On Startup   Checking this is handy if you know you'll be working on the same project over many sessions and prefer to have it open and available on the storyboard or timeline waiting for you. If you leave it unchecked, Movie Maker 2 will start with an empty storyboard or timeline each time you open it. The default is an unchecked box.

Save AutoRecover Info Every *nn* Minutes   The default is 10 minutes, and you can change it to anything from 1 through 60 minutes. Movie Maker automatically backs up the current state of your collection database and the currently open project file. The backup copy is automatically deleted when you close Movie Maker normally. An abnormal closure of Movie Maker, such as a power failure, will result in you being given the option of recovering the state of your project when it was last automatically saved. One caveat: when Movie Maker saves the AutoRecover information, it checks through the entire collection database and the currently open project, backing up everything in case of an abnormal situation such as a power failure. When it does this, it stops normal work. If your collections and

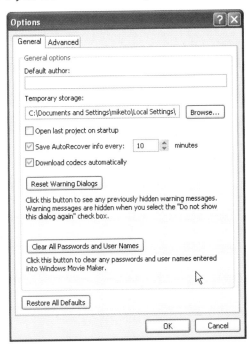

Figure 4-1 The General tab shows you some settings that affect the overall behavior of Movie Maker.

project are small, you might never notice this. For now, leave it at 10 minutes, but if your project collections grow large, you might want to make the time interval longer. You can also uncheck the option so it doesn't function.

Download Codecs Automatically   When you import an audio or video source file but don't have the proper codec, Movie Maker will attempt to get it from the Microsoft Movie Maker Web site. The default is a checked box.

> TIP
>
> If you have an earlier version of Windows Media Player, you'll need to download a special update that contains the Movie Maker 2 codecs. See the Appendix for details on downloading the special update.

Reset Warning Dialogs   When a warning pops up while using Movie Maker 2, it'll have a check box so you can turn off the notification in the future. If you select this option, you'll turn on all warning notifications.

Clear All Passwords And User Names   Click this button to reset all user names and passwords that have been entered and stored in Movie Maker 2. The only place Movie Maker requires user names and passwords is when you save your movie to an online video hosting provider. User names and passwords prevent unauthorized access to your hosting provider, so if you're not using one, clicking this button won't do any harm.

Restore All Defaults   This button restores the defaults for the General tab only. If you want all defaults restored, you'll also need to click the same button on the Advanced tab.

The only option to be particularly careful of on this page is the Default Author setting. If you make up something really cute and forget you put it there, you might end up getting a call when someone watches your movie and sees your cute signature. It's something you might not remember to review before you burn a bunch of discs to distribute your movies. You can always leave it blank and include your name in each project's properties (see Figure 4-2).

You can set these properties by clicking File | Properties and then filling in the desired information in the fields. Click OK. The information in these fields overrides the name you set on the General tab.

The Advanced tab contains the other options that affect all your projects, and because of the way you work with pictures, images, and transitions, you might find yourself setting these options more frequently than the ones on the General tab. Click the Advanced tab, and you should see a dialog box that looks like Figure 4-3.

The Advanced options are as follows:

Picture Duration   Still pictures don't have a duration when they're on your computer as source files or as clips in your collections. This is the option where you get to define how long the default duration will be for your projects. When you click OK, the new setting takes effect immediately. Note that it doesn't affect images already in your storyboard or timeline, only the images in your existing collections. The minimum duration is one-eighth of a second (0.125 seconds), and the maximum is 30 seconds. You can always extend the duration to something longer in the timeline.

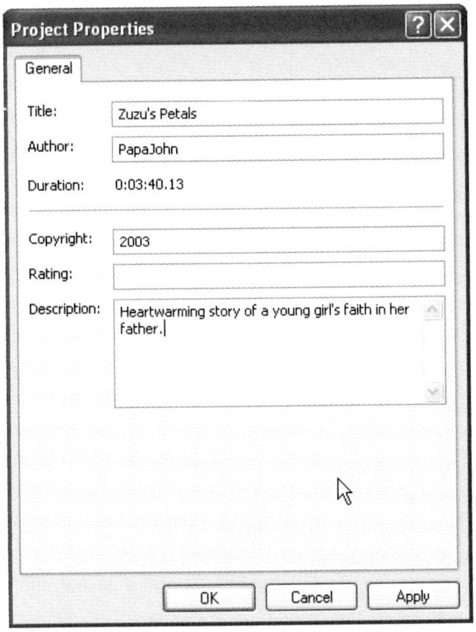

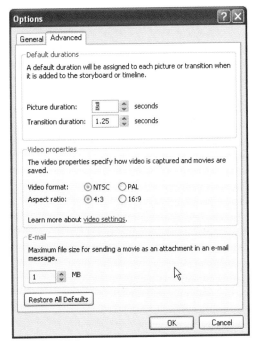

Figure 4-2 The Project Properties dialog box lets you include personal information in each of your projects.

Figure 4-3 The Advanced tab lets you set features such as image duration and transition duration.

Transition Duration Similar to the still picture duration, this setting determines the default time length for any duration applied to the storyboard or timeline. The minimum is one-fourth of a second, and the maximum is the default of five seconds. As with still images, this setting takes effect immediately but doesn't affect any transitions already in the storyboard or timeline.

Video Format The video format is used when recording a movie back to a camcorder. The format is determined by the country or region you're in because television monitors use one or the other to display video images. Generally speaking, North America uses NTSC, and much of Europe (but not all) uses PAL. If Movie Maker can't automatically detect the video format from your camera or from the Regional and Language Option settings in the Control Panel, you might need to select the correct format. For more information about the video format used by your camera, consult the documentation provided with your camera.

Aspect Ratio This specifies the aspect ratio for your saved movies. The setting you choose determines the aspect ratio, which is the relationship between the width and the height of the video display. If you select 4:3 as the aspect ratio, the settings you can choose from when saving your movie include those that have a width-to-height ratio of 4:3. If you select 16:9, the settings you can choose from when saving a movie include those that have a width-to-height ratio of 16:9. Many newer televisions including those designated as HDTV or HDTV-ready, use 16:9, and all older televisions use 4:3. Video converted between the two aspect ratios might cause the final saved movie to appear distorted during playback.

E-Mail This sets the maximum file size when sending a movie as an e-mail attachment, but this setting is sneakier than it sounds. It sets an e-mail file size limit and also causes Movie Maker to select the best settings for saving your movie based on its content, the duration, and the finished file size. This is one default setting you'll want to change; a 1-megabyte (MB) setting creates a movie that's not very good looking. If you want a decent-quality movie sent as an attachment, figure on roughly 2 MB for each minute of finished video. If you're sending a two-and-a-half-minute movie, set the e-mail file size to 5 MB. You can override the setting later just before you save your movie file if your movie is longer or shorter than your planned size. The default setting is 1 MB, and it can go up to 10 MB.

It's always tempting to send movies to friends, family, and relatives by e-mail, but most e-mail providers place limits on the size of files you can send or receive. If your provider only allows files of 5 MB, you might get an error notice saying the message couldn't be delivered. Ask your provider if there are any limits before you send a movie by e-mail.

Restore All Defaults   This button restores the defaults for the Advanced tab only. If you want all defaults restored, you'll also need to click the same button on the General tab.

Organizing Your Projects

Movie Maker holds and organizes all the pieces that make up your final movie: source files, clips, collections, projects, and finished movies. Some kind of organization is best, but the methods for storing and keeping track of your source files, projects, and saved movies can vary from person to person.

This section describes how Movie Maker works with these pieces and offers suggestions on how you can improve your ability to create movies using just a little bit of foresight and organization. Thankfully, there are no rules or "you must do this" instructions; you can do as much or as little of this as you like. Take what works, and leave the rest. And don't forget to have fun!

SETTING UP PRIVACY AND MULTIPLE USERS

Are you the only one making movies on this computer? Or do you share your computer with other family members or friends? Are you wondering if someone can sneak in and start working on your project when you're not around? Not to worry—Movie Maker and Windows XP work together to help keep each user's files separate and private.

Each computer user gets a private folder and storage area on the computer, and personal items in these folders are hidden from other users who don't have administrator privileges. Movie Maker automatically creates and maintains a new database file for each user and treats the movie database and related files as personal items. All the information that Movie Maker knows about your personal collections of source file clips and the related source files themselves is stored in a personal database file that it automatically maintained for you. By default, your database, source files, and project files end up in your My Documents folder, and your saved movie files end up in your My Videos folder. This keeps your files secure and private between different users, so you don't accidentally delete each other's collections or goof up someone's project. If the user with a limited account opens Movie Maker and tries to access a file in another user's account, the error message shown in Figure 4-4 will pop up.

If you want multiple users to work on the same movie, it's best to set up a new account in Windows XP and have everyone work on the movie using that account. By using this method you can have a Movie Studio account for jointly developed movie projects and still keep your personal account available for when you want to work on your own projects.

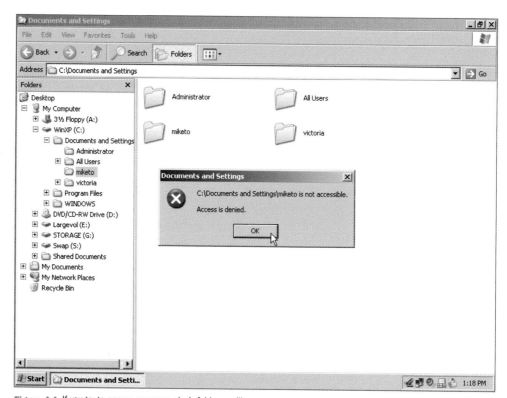

Figure 4-4 If you try to access someone else's folder, you'll see an error message.

BUILD A VIDEO RESOURCE LIBRARY

Even with the prices of big, fast hard disks dropping, it can still be expensive to stuff your computer full of enough hard disks to store all the source files you want to use for your Movie Maker projects.

The way out of this is to be clever about which source files you want to use and when you plan to use them. Think through the long-term needs for the clips. If you think of video clips in a modular way, you can be discerning about what footage remains on your computer for extended periods. This also gives you the starting point for building a video resource library—an offline collection of source files, projects, and finished movies that you can draw upon at any time for your next project.

Collections			
Video Effects			
Video Transitions			
Collections			
⊟ Current Projects			
⊞ Cinderella			
⊞ EIC			
Genealogy			
⊞ Home Video Files to Sort			
⊞ Maui Vacation			
Text Only			
Vacation Perspectives			
Library of Standard Clips			
⊞ Music			

Collection: Vacation Perspectives
Drag a clip and drop it on the timeline below.

Name	Duration	Start Time	End Time
Car Leaving	0:00:03	1:05:33	1:05:36
Car Leaving 2	0:00:01	1:05:36	1:05:38
Stephen - Mississippi River	0:00:12	1:05:38	1:05:50
Drive to Badlands	0:00:10	1:05:50	1:06:00
Bernadette + Chris at Badlands	0:00:06	1:06:00	1:06:05
Badlands 1	0:00:15	1:06:05	1:06:21
Badlands 2	0:00:05	1:06:21	1:06:25
Badlands 3	0:00:03	1:06:25	1:06:28
Badlands - Saddle Pass	0:00:05	1:06:28	1:06:33
Bernadette + 3	0:00:06	1:06:33	1:06:39
Bernadette + Chris	0:00:06	1:06:39	1:06:45
3 Kids	0:00:09	1:06:45	1:06:54
Badlands 4	0:00:04	1:06:54	1:06:59
Bernadette - Badlands	0:00:09	1:06:59	1:07:07
Bernadette + Chis - Badlands	0:00:07	1:07:07	1:07:14
Bernadette - Badlands 2	0:00:04	1:07:14	1:07:18
Chris - Badlands	0:00:10	1:07:18	1:07:28
Chris - Badlands 2	0:00:05	1:07:28	1:07:33
Joanne + Chris - Badlands	0:00:14	1:07:33	1:07:47
Badlands 5	0:00:08	1:07:47	1:07:55
3 Kids - Badlands	0:00:06	1:07:55	1:08:01
Joanne - Badlands	0:00:05	1:08:01	1:08:05
Bernadette - Badlands	0:00:05	1:08:05	1:08:10
Joanne + Chris - Badlands	0:00:07	1:08:10	1:08:17
Wall Drugs	0:00:12	1:08:17	1:08:28
Mt Rushmore	0:00:04	1:08:28	1:08:32
Really Small Town	0:00:13	1:08:32	1:08:45
Joanne Eating on Car	0:00:06	1:08:45	1:08:51
Chris + Stephen - Fireworks	0:00:07	1:08:51	1:08:59

You can pick through your video footage and keep only the clips you really need for future use.

For example, if you've caught the video bug, you're probably shooting film like crazy. But rather than importing every last second of footage onto your computer in hopes of using it someday, *save the camcorder tapes instead.* Don't record over them or reuse them. These are irreplaceable sources; once they're gone, they're really gone. You can always go back to them as source tapes for footage. These are the first pillars in your video resource library.

Next, be selective about what you want to work with and only import what you need. Although Movie Maker offers you the option to import your footage and automatically create clips, take the time to manually go through the raw footage and save each good clip from the tape as an individual DV-AVI file.

After you have a few collections and movies, go through your collections and mentally sort your source files into two groups: those you can use in many projects over the years (beach scenes, air shows, flags blowing, whale-watching trips, flowers, scenery, sunsets, downloaded movies from the Internet) and those with a one-time use, such as a wedding or party.

Collections		Collection: Vacation Perspectives Drag a clip and drop it on the timeline below.			
Video Effects		Name	Duration	Start Time	End Time
Video Transitions		Car Leaving	0:00:03	1:05:33	1:05:36
Collections		Car Leaving 2	0:00:01	1:05:36	1:05:38
Current Projects		Badlands 1	0:00:15	1:06:05	1:06:21
Cinderella		Badlands 2	0:00:05	1:06:21	1:06:25
Genealogy		Badlands 3	0:00:03	1:06:25	1:06:28
Maui Vacation		Badlands - Saddle Pass	0:00:05	1:06:28	1:06:33
Vacation Perspectives		Badlands 4	0:00:04	1:06:54	1:06:59
Bernadette		Badlands 5	0:00:08	1:07:47	1:07:55
Chris		Wall Drugs	0:00:12	1:08:17	1:08:28
Joanne		Mt Rushmore	0:00:04	1:08:28	1:08:32
John		Really Small Town	0:00:13	1:08:32	1:08:45
Stephen		Mountains	0:00:19	1:09:19	1:09:38
Planned Projects		Mountains	0:00:07	1:10:06	1:10:14
Library of Standard Clips		Car and mountains	0:00:05	1:10:14	1:10:18
Movies Being Distributed		Driving Through Mountains	0:00:17	1:10:18	1:10:35
Archived Projects		Grand Tetons - Resort	0:00:05	1:10:35	1:10:41
Music		Snake River	0:00:10	1:11:38	1:11:47
		Horses	0:00:18	1:11:56	1:12:14
		Mountain Stream	0:00:03	1:12:20	1:12:23
		Mountain Stream	0:00:09	1:12:23	1:12:32
		Animal	0:00:08	1:12:32	1:12:39
		Mountain Trail	0:00:09	1:12:44	1:12:54

After you have weeded out old clips, you can sort them into the proper collections.

For scenes that have potential reuse value in projects over the years, carve them up into the smallest individual clips you can, save them as individual DV-AVI files, burn them to CDs or DVDs, and then erase the clips from your hard disk. A three-minute DV-AVI clip, which can fit onto a CD, isn't very long for traditional viewing but is a pretty long clip for editing purposes. Once these clips are on CDs, with notes in a database about what and where they are, you can copy them back onto your computer as needed for movie projects and then import them back into Movie Maker.

These offline video resource libraries are a handy way of keeping images, clips, transitions, and source files available without gobbling up hard disk space. These CD and DVD collections are the second pillars in your video resource library.

For the footage with a one-time use, discard the source clips about three months after the movie has been distributed and you haven't touched the project since. You should still save the movie, but you probably don't need the footage from Aunt Millie's seventy-fifth birthday party permanently on your hard disk. Your saved movies are the third pillars in your resource library; plus, they have something extra: they're *your* movies, stamped with your own personal touch.

In any event, if you want to share source files used by Movie Maker 2, you should store all such files in a shared folder outside the default My Documents or My Videos folder. Windows XP creates a Shared Documents directory that's an ideal place to store the source files and finished videos.

ORGANIZING SOURCE FILES

Working with source files comes in two general categories: how to organize them and where to store them. These go hand in hand because how you decide to organize your files helps determine where you'll store them. The answers might surprise you; stick around for some interesting ideas you can use to help get better organized.

For most people, organization is something that's usually done long after it should've been started, after you realize you're spending more time looking for files than you are working with them. There's no better time to get started than right now!

Source files can be just about anything you can import into Movie Maker. Movie Maker doesn't make copies of these files but uses them while you build your movie. So although Movie Maker gives you one way of organizing your source files, you should also do some housework by keeping the files organized on your hard disk.

TIP

You can filter your collections by any of the collection headings in Detail view. Click a heading and you can sort in ascending or descending order. This helps you find a clip of a certain length or size or by the date created.

You can organize your source files in a number of ways, depending on how you work and what works best for you. Because source files are stored in folders, your organization will follow some method of placing your source files in appropriate folders and subfolders. The naming and arrangement of the folders can be by the following:

Movie or project type   Each movie gets its own folder.

File types   Video clips, pictures, music, narration, or audio.

Topic or theme   Vacations, work, scenic, or events.

Date   Year, month, or video capture date.

People   Immediate family, relatives, or friends.

You can try different methods or even use combinations of these methods. For example, you could create folders for each movie and then store the source files by file type within that folder. The goal is to make it easier to find your source files, not to increase your workload or frustrate you when you try to find a particular image or source file. Figure 4-5 shows you one example that lists current movie projects with subcollections for tapes and clips.

So much for *how* to store your source files. *Where* to store files is a fun topic to work with because the storage possibilities offer new ways to organize your files.

Video source files can be huge. An hour of high-quality DV-AVI files uses about 13 gigabytes (GB) of space. You'll want to have your video source files on your computer during a project but will want to delete them when the project is completed. And, of course, you'll have a number of projects working in parallel, so you might have a significant portion of your hard disk devoted to your video source files.

If you have the money or just like having the biggest, fattest computer on the block, you can install multiple hard disks in your computer. The Appendix goes into more detail on the benefits and what to look for in storage devices. If you have a computer acting as a server on your network, you can use that server as the repository for your source files. You can also use DVDs as offline storage solutions for files of 4 GB or so, which can give you virtually inexhaustible storage, limited only by your pocketbook and the amount of room in your home. However, both DVDs and CDs are quite slow for importing clips, so they're best for short clip storage rather than complete collections of raw footage or finished movies.

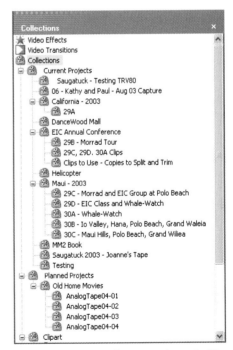

ORGANIZING CLIPS

Because you'll be working with all kinds of clips in each project, a few clip-keeping suggestions will go a long way to making your movie-making process easy.

When you first import video and create clips from the source file, the clip names start with the name of the source file you imported. But you're free to change the clip names to whatever best suits your movie-making needs. It's best that

Figure 4-5 When your projects are neatly organized like this, it makes it easy to find the clip you want to use.

they have nice, short, descriptive names before you bring them into your movie projects. You can also move clips from one collection to another or copy them from one collection and paste them into another. You can have as many copies of a clip as you want in a collection or in any number of collections.

Pictures from digital still cameras often have sequential numbers assigned by the camera. Clips from video files, when automatically cut into smaller clips, will all have the same name, with sequential number suffixes. Sequential numbers don't tell you much about the clip; if you haven't already, spend some time renaming them. Ideally, you'll want to use names that match the content or something that stands out about the clip, rather than naming clips for how you plan to use them in a project.

Music seems best suited to having collections that parallel your music CDs, with the clips in each collection being the pieces on the album.

ORGANIZING COLLECTIONS

Being smart about how you organize your collections is the easiest, most powerful way you can enhance Movie Maker. The huge advantages to organizing your collections properly are as follows:

- Your system reflects the way you think, making it easier to find what you want.

- Your system is flexible, allowing you to mix, match, and copy clips as needed to meet project needs.

- Your system grows and changes as your projects increase with the fun and creativity you have working with Movie Maker.

As with source files and clips, you can organize your collections in just about any order you want. One of the most flexible is to have some of your collections named after the themes, ideas, topics, or subjects you've filmed and imported into Movie Maker, with others named after specific projects or movies you're making. This lets you have collections that are clear about what they contain because of their names: for example, Kids, Scenery, Museums, Dolphins, Classical Music, and Unusual Buildings. So when you need a clip that contains just the right outdoor background, you can find one without trying to think which movie you used it in or what the filename was. Figure 4-6 shows you a listing of clips based on content.

You can further organize your collections by adding subcollections, by renaming collections, by moving them drag-and-drop style from one place to another, or by deleting them. Movie Maker always lists your collections in alphabetical order in a fully expanded state, so each time you start Movie Maker you see all your collections in the tree at once.

One quirk about collections is that Movie Maker lists them in alphabetical order only; you can't list them by date created, by size, or by any other detail. This can be a problem if your latest movie project is called "Zuzu's Petals" because it'll appear at the bottom of the Collections tree. It gets old scrolling down to the bottom of the list every time you want to select clips for use in the timeline.

Collection: 29D – Boarding and Dolphins
Drag a clip and drop it on the timeline below.

Name	Duration	St...	End Time	Dimensions	Date Taken
Dock and Boats	0:00:25	0:05:31	0:05:57	320 x 240	4/18/2003 4:25 PM
People on Dock	0:00:32	0:05:57	0:06:28	320 x 240	4/18/2003 4:25 PM
Boarding	0:00:33	0:06:28	0:07:01	320 x 240	4/18/2003 4:25 PM
Other Boats	0:00:39	0:07:01	0:07:40	320 x 240	4/18/2003 4:25 PM
Bernadette Taking Pix	0:00:15	0:07:40	0:07:55	320 x 240	4/18/2003 4:25 PM
Looking for Whales	0:00:28	0:07:55	0:08:23	320 x 240	4/18/2003 4:25 PM
Boat - Group	0:00:22	0:08:23	0:08:45	320 x 240	4/18/2003 4:25 PM
29D (3)	0:00:39	0:08:45	0:09:24	320 x 240	4/18/2003 4:25 PM
29D (2)	0:02:34	0:09:24	0:11:58	320 x 240	4/18/2003 4:25 PM
Spinner Dolphin and Boat	0:00:35	0:11:58	0:12:33	320 x 240	4/18/2003 4:25 PM
29D (4)	0:00:12	0:12:33	0:12:45	320 x 240	4/18/2003 4:25 PM
Dolphins and Spinner	0:00:17	0:12:45	0:13:01	320 x 240	4/18/2003 4:25 PM
Boat and Dolphins	0:00:38	0:13:01	0:13:40	320 x 240	4/18/2003 4:25 PM
29D (5)	0:00:24	0:13:40	0:14:04	320 x 240	4/18/2003 4:25 PM
Nice Dolphins with Our Boat	0:00:14	0:14:04	0:14:18	320 x 240	4/18/2003 4:25 PM
Dolphins With Our Boat	0:00:20	0:14:18	0:14:38	320 x 240	4/18/2003 4:25 PM
Watching	0:00:04	0:19:10	0:19:14	320 x 240	4/18/2003 4:25 PM
Whales - 2	0:00:10	0:19:14	0:19:24	320 x 240	4/18/2003 4:25 PM
Whale Body	0:00:21	0:21:00	0:21:21	320 x 240	4/18/2003 4:25 PM
Tails and Spouts	0:00:39	0:21:21	0:22:00	320 x 240	4/18/2003 4:25 PM
29D (1)	0:00:54	0:22:30	0:23:24	320 x 240	4/18/2003 4:25 PM
Nice Tail	0:00:10	0:23:24	0:23:34	320 x 240	4/18/2003 4:25 PM
29D (7)	0:01:27	0:23:34	0:25:01	320 x 240	4/18/2003 4:25 PM
Big Nice Tail	0:00:23	0:25:01	0:25:24	320 x 240	4/18/2003 4:25 PM
Bodies	0:02:24	0:25:24	0:27:48	320 x 240	4/18/2003 4:25 PM
29D (6)	0:01:43	0:27:48	0:29:30	320 x 240	4/18/2003 4:25 PM
Big and Close Tail	0:00:10	0:29:30	0:29:40	320 x 240	4/18/2003 4:25 PM
29D (9)	0:02:58	0:29:40	0:32:38	320 x 240	4/18/2003 4:25 PM
Whale and Start of Good Narrative	0:00:59	0:32:38	0:33:37	320 x 240	4/18/2003 4:25 PM
More Narrative	0:01:20	0:33:37	0:34:57	320 x 240	4/18/2003 4:25 PM
Nice Tail	0:00:26	0:34:57	0:35:23	320 x 240	4/18/2003 4:25 PM
Heads and Bodies	0:00:22	0:35:23	0:35:45	320 x 240	4/18/2003 4:25 PM
Two Tails - Almost	0:00:47	0:37:25	0:38:12	320 x 240	4/18/2003 4:25 PM
Narrative Toward End	0:03:07	0:38:12	0:41:20	320 x 240	4/18/2003 4:25 PM
Heads, Bodies, Tails	0:01:20	0:41:20	0:42:39	320 x 240	4/18/2003 4:25 PM

Figure 4-6 If you name your collections based on content, you can find relevant clips quickly and view them to see if they are appropriate.

The way around this is to be sneaky about how you name your collections. Creative naming includes using leading spaces to move the collection up to the top of the tree, even if the name begins with the letter "Z." Figure 4-7 shows one arrangement of collections that places the more current projects high in the tree and the least used one last, even though the last one starts with the letter "A." A double leading space moves an item above a single leading space, regardless of what letter it starts with. So name your projects using a leading space (or two leading spaces), and Movie Maker will pop your project to the top of the tree.

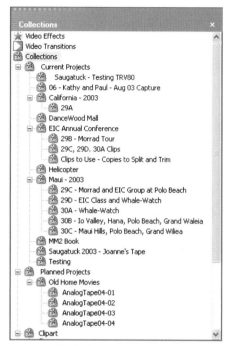

Figure 4-7 Use leading spaces to put your project names at the top of the collection tree.

Don't forget the great option of copying and pasting to put the most frequently used collections within your latest project. For example, if you're starting a holiday movie project and you have a collection full of holiday-themed clips or transitions and effects, copy the special collection into the new project. The holiday collection will be close to the clips of your new project, making it a lot easier to drag clips to the timeline without a lot of scrolling up and down the Collections tree. When the project is done, you can simply delete the extra folder under the project.

ORGANIZING PROJECTS

Your project files are those with the .MSWMM extension. By default they're in your My Videos folder, and each of your movies will have its own project file. When you click File | Save Project As, you name your project and create the MSWMM file. All the information needed about the clips and their source files has been copied from the collection database into the project file. You can now open the project file, do more editing, and even make the video from the project files, without the collections you created during the movie-making process. As long as your source files are available, you only need the project file to re-edit or do a complete build of the movie.

The best way to save your project files is by creating a subfolder under My Videos for your project files so you can easily drill down to a particular project and the movie you've been working on. This also has the side benefit of having them all in a single location for ease of use and backing up.

Projects aren't necessarily all about an entire movie or finished product for your friends and family. For instance, if you have a really neat set of clips that you used for the opening scene of a previous movie, complete with special effects, transitions, text, and narration, you should create a new project, copy the set of clips and everything else into the new project, and then save the project. You now have a project that consists solely of your opening sequence that you can reuse in other movies by copying and pasting the sequence into yet another project. Why reinvent the wheel if you don't have to?

ORGANIZING SAVED MOVIES

Your saved movies from Movie Maker 2 will vary in size from the highest-quality DV-AVI files to the much smaller compressed ones used as e-mail attachments. The space that a movie file uses and the options you have to save such large files are your constraints. Between the video capture source files and your finished movies, these are the two primary "disk space hogs" you'll encounter while you create more and better movies.

As discussed in the source files section, there's no easy way out of the storage space dilemma. The main organization suggestion is easy: either delete your finished movies or move them off your computer's hard disk to another storage medium. If you have a digital camcorder, you can make a copy of the highest-quality movies by saving them back to a camcorder tape. A digital camcorder tape can hold an hour of video and is the most economical storage option. Burning movies to DVD is sometimes, but not always, an option; movies of any substantial length will exceed even the storage space of DVDs.

There's a third option available: you can reclaim the hard disk space consumed by the finished movies by keeping copies of the source and project files on your computer so you can render another movie copy if you need to do so. This is the most flexible option because you can render movies using different settings for different hardware devices; see Chapter 5 for more information about saving movies. The compromise is that you still have the source files on your hard disk, but if you're smart about which source files you keep on your computer (see the section on source files), you might be able to offload some of those, thus saving you even more hard disk space.

CAPTURE AND PRESERVE OLD MOVIES

This isn't the first time that making home videos has been popular. In the early sixties through the early seventies, many people invested in film cameras that shot footage on 8mm film. Actual 8mm film had no room for an audio track, while "Super 8" film developed by Kodak used advances in sprocket size and placement to squeeze an audio track onto the film. Both types of film were developed and played back on projectors. Basic editing could be done using an 8mm film splicer and some cellophane tape or special glue, such as you see here. The movie quality was about what you would expect, but for its time it was a way for many to capture special events or vacations without hiring professionals with bulky lights and equipment.

If you have any old movies like these that your family took when you were a kid, or that you took yourself, you can help preserve the film footage by transferring it to digital format. As film ages, it becomes brittle, the film chemicals oxidize, and the colors become muddied and less brilliant. When you transfer your footage to digital, you "stop" the aging process before it progresses too far.

Old-school film editing used tools like this splicer, tape, and glue.

One way you can capture the footage is to set up an 8mm projector and screen, play the reels, and film the movies using your digital camera set up on a tripod or other stable surface. Make a couple of test runs to see how the footage turns out. You may need to move the digital camera closer or farther away from the screen, in combination with using the zoom and focus, to get the best clarity you can. You can also adjust exposures and settings on the digital camera to capture as much color and depth of field as possible.

You can capture old film by projecting then "reshooting" it with your digital camera.

If there is audio on the original film, you may need to do some additional work. If you play back the audio track along with the film, you will pick up the clatter of the projector gate; this will most likely drown out most of the sounds you are looking to capture. Some projectors have an "audio out" RCA jack meant for an external speaker. You could try placing the speaker in a different room and recording the audio separately with your video camera. Don't hook the projector and your camera up directly unless you know for sure they are compatible and use compatible line voltages.

You may also be able to find a specialty store in your neighborhood or on the Internet that will do the transfer for you. They have sophisticated facilities and will be able to capture the video and audio in the best possible condition.

And, of course, at some point you might as well invest in another, larger hard disk. The Appendix has information to help you know what to buy.

Finally, you should start keeping a log, spreadsheet, or personal database of all your movie work. You should create a record for each project file, with notes about the source files and project files used, what movies were built from it, how they were distributed, and where the offline files are kept.

Rounding Up Source Files and Importing Them

You won't use Movie Maker 2 to obtain your still image or audio files or to convert them to appropriate formats or sizes for use in your movies. But there are some rules of thumb you can use when rounding them up. This section gives you an overview of some of the usual methods and appropriate comments for the different sources and importing the files into Movie Maker 2:

Online files   Once you've downloaded these files or saved images to your hard disk, you can usually import them directly into Movie Maker. If in doubt about the ability of Movie Maker to use it, test it.

Music from CDs   Movie Maker can't directly use the files on your audio CDs, but you can use the Windows Media Player or other software to copy them from the CD to your computer.

NOTE

The Movie Maker online help lists the file extensions for file types that can be imported. This list is constantly being updated, depending on the codecs available from Microsoft or from third-party software developers. When in doubt, check with Microsoft or with other developer sites to see if a new format has recently been added to the list. You can also check *http://www.papajohn.org* for discussions and latest news about additional supported formats.

Video from DVDs and video CDs   Unless they contain easily used WMV files, copying video clips from such sources are sometimes fairly complex computer tasks. Saving all or part of a movie from a CD or DVD will require other software, and because of copy protection technology, you might not be able to save a copy to your hard disk at all. Assuming you can make a copy, you'll probably need to convert the file to a usable format before importing into Movie Maker. If the other software gives you a choice about saved-file quality, select the highest-quality file you can get from such sources.

Digital camcorders   If you have the hard disk space, capture your video clips in DV-AVI format for the highest-quality inputs to your movies.

Analog video devices   Capturing video from analog devices such as VCRs, TVs, and certain camcorders requires specialized hardware or software that usually doesn't come with a computer. If you have a video capture card or audio card with video input, you probably have a software package that came with the card that will grab the files for use in Movie Maker. Again, aim for high-quality DV-AVI files.

Web cams   Web cams are small cameras that can be connected to your computer using a parallel port, a Universal Serial Bus (USB) connection, and so on. You might need special software to get the still pictures or video from such cameras; most Web cams come with an image-grabbing program that can take movies or pictures automatically, on a regular schedule, or even manually, just like a regular camcorder. See the software instructions to discover which formats it supports.

Scanners   A great way to get old photo album pictures, textures from items or material around the house, or unusual images from old books into your computer is by using a flatbed scanner. These scanners almost always have specialized programs that can scan various resolutions and various types of images. This might sound like a broken record, but take the highest resolution and best-quality scanned image that you can. You can reduce it, crop it, or resize it later when getting ready to use it as a movie clip.

Digital cameras and still pictures   If you need to prep or convert still images before importing them into Movie Maker 2, aim for 640 × 480 resolution to align with the high-quality video size option when saving your movie. Digital cameras, scanners, and other image-related programs let you choose the image size and color depth (see Figure 4-8). Make the adjustments, and then save the file as a copy; if you save over the original, the original is gone—unless you still have the copy on a memory card or can rescan the original picture.

TIP

When you're working with a digital image, always start with a high-resolution image and save to a lower resolution. This preserves as much of the original image information as possible in the derivative image. If you do the reverse, you're stretching small amounts of information over a larger area, making the image blurry, "jaggy," and fuzzy. Try both methods on a test image and see the difference.

Other applications   Perhaps you create your own source files using software such as Adobe Photoshop or Adobe Premiere or by creating MIDI music from an audio authoring package. There are many computer applications you can use to create new and exciting effects. These files might need to be prepped before you can use them. Still images might need to be cropped and resized to better fit the standard video image sizes and proportions. For example, Movie Maker 2 can handle a 4000 × 3000 pixel image. But, if your movie is long and has many such images, the resources needed to handle them might be more than those needed for more appropriately sized 640 × 480 pixel images.

Figure 4-8 With the right software, digital cameras will let you edit the picture after you've taken it.

Computer-captured video   Maybe you're a computer game player and want to show your friends how you beat your last highest score. You'd like to capture some footage from a game and include it in a movie. Or maybe you're making a Web-based tutorial about how to use Movie Maker 2 and want to make a movie of the screens while you demonstrate it, complete with narration. You'd need to use other software to capture your video clips before importing them into Movie Maker 2. Consider using the Windows Media Encoder package for such items. It uses the same underlying software engine that Movie Maker 2 uses and works well with it. You can download it from *http://www.microsoft.com/ windows/windowsmedia/9series/encoder/default.aspx*. And—repeat along—use the highest-quality capture you can, preferably in DV-AVI format, to ensure the video clips are the highest quality.

Converting Your Source Files

You can capture video files from your camcorder, download them from the Internet, or copy them from a video CD or DVD. You can get still images from your digital camera, your scanner, your artwork in Photoshop, the Internet, or from a friend as an attachment to an e-mail. Many music files will come from CDs. And your audio files might be narrations you recorded or sound effects from the Internet.

But as noted in the previous section, you'll probably need to use other software to capture all the different types of source files, and even then you might not be able to use them directly in Movie Maker. For example, a video clip that was taken by a Sony MicroMV camcorder (which uses the MPEG-2 format) or an Apple QuickTime movie (with a .mov extension) isn't in a suitable format to import into Movie Maker. You must convert these clips first to a supported format by using other software. Movie Maker 2 doesn't do these conversions, so you have to use other software or use innovative methods.

If you need to convert a video file, you should ask yourself a couple of questions. What quality is the video file that you're starting with? What are you planning to do with the clips from it? If you're starting with highly compressed MPEG-2 files and are expecting to make high-quality DVDs from your Movie Maker 2 project, you might have to rethink your options regardless of conversion. It's much better to assess your options up front rather than putting hundreds of hours into editing sessions and finding that you can't make high-quality DVDs from the material simply because the source material wasn't of sufficient quality.

If you have video hardware such as micro-camcorders that output a highly compressed MPEG-2 file, you'll need to use the software that came with your hardware to do the capturing and then use other software to convert it into a format you can import using Movie Maker 2 (see Figure 4-9). Sometimes a video MPEG-1 file will work fine, but an MPEG-2 file won't, or vice versa, because MPEG video files can be encoded using different codecs. The best way to check is to try importing it into Movie Maker. If the import process doesn't work or the file gets imported but behaves strangely, then you'll need to convert it using other software.

Figure 4-9 Some videos may need to be converted before you can import them into Movie Maker 2.

Conversion isn't usually needed for still pictures. Your images are probably already in JPG or BMP formats and ready to import. Sometimes you need to prep still images even if you don't need to convert them. The reasons to do some work on still images include the following:

- Changing the proportions of an image to align with the movie proportions. This is to avoid the black bars at the sides or the top and bottom. This is subjective because some people prefer to use the whole image and aren't concerned about the black bars. The two standard image sizes for Movie Maker are 640 × 480 and 320 × 240, so if you edit your images to these sizes, they'll fit better in the final movie.

- Cropping out the focal point of an image. With the pixel size of a movie usually smaller than that of a still image, you might want to zoom in on the most interesting part of the image and crop it before importing. This saves space and video resources and makes it easier for Movie Maker to compile a movie using that image.

- Enhancing colors, sharpness, or other aspects of a picture is easier and better done in picture imaging software that specializes in such editing, such as Microsoft Picture It. Also, rotating a picture is easily done in image software and will reduce the video resources needed to rotate the same item using a special video effect.

If you need help resolving a compatibility issue with a source file, it's best to check the latest information on the Movie Maker Web site at *http://www.microsoft.com/windowsxp/moviemaker/default.asp*, the book's Web site at *http://www.papajohn.org*, or the Microsoft newsgroup at *microsoft.public.windowsxp.moviemaker*. If you routinely get source files from a particular place, test one fully before putting a lot of work into editing a movie and finding that it won't save properly. Make a short (15-second) movie from it. If the short one works fine, then you can assume that the others will also work well and invest as much effort into editing your movies as you want.

PREP AN IMAGE USING MICROSOFT PAINT

Still pictures of nearly any format, size, and shape will usually work fine in Movie Maker 2. But a bit of preparation before importing the image often enhances the movie, better focuses on the topic, and eliminates black vertical or horizontal areas around the picture.

You can prep an image using one of the basic tools in Windows XP: Microsoft Paint. Paint is a picture creation and manipulation tool. You might have more powerful image editing software available, but for basic preparation Paint will do nicely.

First, check the picture attributes by selecting the Image | Attributes command; it will show you basic information about your image, as shown below. If you need to resize the image, you can type in the pixel dimensions for height and width and then click OK. You can also convert an image to grayscale by clicking the Black and White button.

Resizing can affect the image quality; if you go from a larger size to a smaller one, image quality will be preserved, but if you go from smaller to larger, image quality will degrade. Aspect ratio can also be changed, making figures seem "squatty" or stretched thin. Try working with different heights and widths before you settle on your final image.

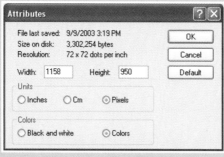

You can resize and grayscale your image by adjusting the image settings in the Attributes dialog box.

Paint also allows you to select and crop areas of the image, change colors, add captions, and work other changes on the image itself; the image on the following page has had a purple background and caption added for later use in Movie Maker. Without going into detail here, you can find out how to do these things by consulting Paint's online help file.

Many sophisticated editing functions are available in Paint, such as adding text captions and changing image backgrounds.

When you work on images, you can save yourself a lot of grief by making a copy of the image first, then working on the copy. That way, if you want to start over, you can make another copy of the original. Paint only remembers the last three changes you made, so for most people clicking Undo won't get back to a clean, unaltered image.

Saving and Backing Up Your Files

You'll start exploring features, and, before you realize it, you'll have invested such a considerable amount of time in a project that you won't want to lose it accidentally. Start your saving and backing up habits now before you get so deeply into the project that you forget. Click the disk icon on the toolbar, click File | Save Project from the menu, or press Ctrl+S. It's never too soon to start good saving habits; you should save early and save often. You should save especially before moving on to a new step.

There's also the AutoRecover automatic saving feature mentioned earlier in this chapter, but don't expect it to be your file saving method. It works simply in cases of a power failure or program freeze during a working session. It doesn't save your current work when everything is working normally. The responsibility for saving your files begins and ends with *you*.

For backing up your files, there are two sets of files you must back up regularly. The first is the Movie Maker database file for each user that contains all the information about your collections and the location of source files and other useful information about your environment and Movie Maker options. You can find it at C:\Documents and Settings\%username%\Local Settings\Application Data\Microsoft\Movie Maker\mediatabx.dat, where *x* is a variable number. Movie Maker 2 doesn't include a feature to automatically back up this file to a safe location, such as burning it onto a CD, so you'll have to hunt down and back up this file yourself.

The other files you should back up regularly are the movie project files, the ones with the MSWMM extension. If you followed the advice earlier in this chapter, you have a subfolder in the My Videos folder that holds all your project files. Each user should have a folder such as this for their own storage, so those will also need to be backed up regularly.

You might have noticed that the critical files to back up are stored in each user's private file area. Unless you have administrator privileges, you normally can't get at those folders to back them up. Take a look at the Windows XP online help files for information about using the backup program and scheduling jobs that run on a recurring basis; it might give you just the tools you need to ensure you don't lose these critical files.

Glossary

BMP
The acronym for "bitmap." This is an image file format that uses a code to describe each pixel in a picture.

codec
Contraction for "encoder/decoder." A codec is a piece of software that encodes and decodes data into an appropriate format. Examples of commonly used codecs are MP3, AVI, and WMA.

HDTV
The acronym for "High-Definition Television." This is a standard that uses much higher resolutions for broadcast and reception and is usually associated with newer televisions and digital equipment.

JPG
Photographic compression format used for still images.

MPEG
The acronym for "Moving Picture Experts Group." This engineering organization develops standards for encoding digital audio and video. Several standards have been proposed and adopted over the years, including MPEG-1, which provided encoding for early digital audio and video (including MP3); MPEG-2, which is most commonly used in DVD and in some cable broadcast systems; and MPEG-4, which is a standard for Web-based digital media.

NTSC
The acronym for "National Television Standards Committee," which is a North American engineering organization that sets technical standards for video equipment, broadcast equipment, and home consumer equipment.

PAL
The acronym for "Phase Alternation Line," which is a European engineering organization that sets technical standards for video equipment, broadcast equipment, and home consumer equipment.

- Compressed vs. Uncompressed Movie Files
- Save Your Movie Using Different Compression Options
- Choose How You Want to Distribute Your Movie
- Burn Your Movies to DVD Format

Sharing Your Movies

CHAPTER 5

Do you prefer higher quality in your movies so they look and sound better, or would you rather have smaller file sizes for ease of distribution? Yes, we all prefer both! This chapter is all about balancing these often-conflicting desires.

The options are pretty straightforward and simple to choose when you save your movie.

Coming Attractions

Creating and playing your movies on your computer can be fun, but it's only one of the ways you can share your new creations with friends and family. Depending on who your audience is and what they'll be using to view your movie, Windows Movie Maker 2 offers you several different options for creating your movie and distributing it, anywhere from an e-mail message to CD or DVD to the Internet.

In this chapter, you'll learn about the different distribution methods available, how those methods affect your choice of movie quality, and how to distribute your movie using the Internet to eager friends and family.

Compressed vs. Uncompressed Files

Before getting into actual distribution methods, it's important to understand the difference between compressed files and uncompressed ones. In a nutshell, it's the difference between lower quality and smaller files vs. higher quality and bigger files. If you want smaller files that you can distribute over the Internet or that you can send by e-mail, your movie will be smaller on the screen and play back at lower quality. Movie Maker lets you strike a balance between the two, and once you understand the differences, you can make smart choices about picture quality and file size. In many cases, you might not be able to see the differences in quality between them. Because nothing is ever truly "final" as long as you have your project file and source files available, you can always try different options to see how they look.

The most commonly used and flexible option is to use the Microsoft Windows Media Video (WMV) file format, which can be played back by Windows Media Player. Both Movie Maker 2 and Media Player 9 use a codec that does a great job of compressing and playing back video. The compressed files take up much less room than other formats and play back with high quality, depending on your choices during the movie-saving process. WMV files are good choices for the following reasons:

High-quality movies for playback on your computer When you're saving movies for playback on your own computer, Movie Maker makes some optimization choices that give you the best possible playback quality. If there's room on your hard disk for your movie collection, you can watch any of the WMV files at any time without having to resave the movie.

A short movie to send as an e-mail attachment Most e-mail attachments should be small anyway because of e-mail attachment restrictions set by Internet service providers (ISPs). Movies, even compressed ones, take up a lot of space and take a long time to download, even over high-speed Internet connections.

Web sites for file downloading or streaming When you download a movie file, it's saved to your computer and is available for playback at any time. Streaming video servers play the movie each time the viewer wants to see it, but the receiving computer doesn't save a copy to view later.

HighMAT CDs, the ones automatically burned by Movie Maker 2 These CDs use a computer-generated menu structure to navigate the WMV files on it. It's a great choice for playback on computers that run Windows XP. Even if a computer can't see the HighMAT menu, it might be able to play the individual WMV files on it. Windows Media Player versions newer than 7.01 can play the version 9 WMV files using Windows 98, Me, 2000, or XP. As of mid-2003, there were no DVD players available to view the HighMAT CDs on TVs, and there were no firm projections of when they would be available.

> You can use conversion software to convert a WMV file to another format; see Chapter 4 for information about file conversion. It's best to compress a file directly into a particular format than to render it to one format and convert it to another. Otherwise you'll lose some video and audio information while the movie goes through several compression/decompression/conversion sequences.
>
> **NOTE**

Your other option for compression is Digital Video–Audio Video Interleave (DV-AVI) format. The DV-AVI files are the highest-quality ones you can produce using Movie Maker, but they're also the biggest files, the most difficult to manage on your hard disk, and the hardest to distribute. They appeal to those who want the highest quality and are willing to do the extra computer work required to achieve it. If you choose to save to a digital video (DV) camera, this format is chosen automatically. It's also available as a selectable option when you save to another location, such as your local computer.

A DV-AVI movie is a good choice for the following reasons:

Saving your movie to your hard disk to use in further editing sessions If you have standard clips you'll be using for all your movies, such as introductions or closing credits, you can use this format, import it back into another project, and edit it as needed. It's also a good format if you're going to use the footage in a higher-end editing program for specialized editing or transition needs, such as Adobe Premiere (*http://www.adobe.com/products/premiere/*). The DV-AVI format lets you work on the same file in both applications and maintain the highest quality.

Creating a high-quality video CD or DVD Movie Maker doesn't create DVDs automatically, so you'll need to use another software package to create and burn a DVD with your videos on it. If you want to use other packages and maintain optimal quality at each step, save your movie to your hard disk in DV-AVI format and then use it as a source file for the other software.

Exporting your movie back to your digital camcorder Movie Maker will automatically use the DV-AVI format.

Typically, when you save your movies, you won't need to think much about these different formats. For the most part, your choice as the movie's creator and editor is to select an appropriate degree of compression to balance the file size and quality with your distribution options and methods.

With this background and understanding of the differences between uncompressed DV-AVI and compressed WMV files—and the appropriate times to use them—you can more easily select the options in the wizard while you step through the various methods of saving your movies.

You've Made Your Movie, Now Save It

You've been saving your movie *project* between editing sessions. How do you then make a *movie* from it? While you edited and fine-tuned your movie, you watched the progress in the Movie Maker video monitor. By watching the movie in the preview monitor, you might have thought that the project itself was the movie; did you feel a bit curious about whether your movie would look just like that when you finally saved your movie? No, the preview is just that—a preview of what the movie will look like, but without all the necessary conversion and compression codecs to create the final product. Your movie will actually look much better after you've saved it and when you view it on a true video player.

To save the movie itself, you don't have to do much more than tell Movie Maker how you'd like to distribute it. It's as easy as picking one of five distribution methods and then selecting options from each of the Save Movie Wizard screens while you step through them.

The process of making a movie file from your project is called "rendering." When you finish with the wizard, Movie Maker will render the movie to a temporary file on your hard disk, building it piece by piece while it gets the details from your source files and puts them together in accordance with the design in your project file.

The rendering process takes a lot of time and computer energy. Even with a powerful computer, it might take two to three times the movie's running time to render the temporary file. And during that time, most of the computer's energy will be devoted to it, slowing it down for other tasks. When the rendering is finished, Movie Maker will copy the newly created movie file from its temporary file to the destination you selected. Finally, when it's finished with the rendering process, Movie Maker will clean up by deleting the temporary file.

> When Movie Maker estimates how much space it needs on your hard disk, it projects the final size of the movie file but doesn't include the needed "elbow room" the file will need. This accounts for some disparity between the estimate and the actual space the file occupies on your hard disk.

TIP

EXPLORE DIFFERENT
PERSPECTIVES ONLINE

When considering distribution of your movies, don't limit yourself to one method. For example, in Chapter 1, you learned how to get differing perspectives of your vacation; the project started with the assumption that your goal was to produce a CD or DVD with everyone's movie on it so you could share it easily with everyone via your computer or TV set, or ship the disc off to relatives so they could share the fun. But think about another way of sharing different perspectives: putting the videos online, complete with Web pages and links to additional material that isn't included in the video. This gives you and your family and friends even more creative freedom to tell your stories. Of course, it'll require different options when saving the movies.

Sat - 6/14/80 - day 2 - Rockford to Souix Falls, South Dakota - left Rockford only an hour behind schedule. Noted that we had lost a wheel cover. Had to do Wisconsin and 500 miles today. Stopped at the <u>Mississippi River</u> for lunch and got to Souix Falls about 8 PM.

Sun - 6/15/80 - day 3 - Souix Falls to Lusk, Wyoming - left Souix Falls at 10 AM, an hour late. 475 miles planned for today, stopping at <u>Wall Drug</u> store for lunch (signs have been advertising it already for 100's of miles now). But we have to cross the <u>Badlands</u> first, and then the black hills. A short stop at <u>Mt Rushmore</u> in the evening. Then on to Lusk, one of the bigger towns. We sure had passed through some <u>pretty small</u> ones on the way.

Mon - 6/16/80 - day 4 - Lusk to the Grand Tetons - everyone sacrificed breaks (except for the fireworks) to travel into the <u>Rocky Mountains</u> and <u>get to</u> the Grand Teton lodge. Got there about 5:30. Everyone instantly loved it, and the kids started <u>feeding the gophers</u>. So we immediately reserved an extra day, dropping one of the planned days in San Franciso.

Tues - 6/17/80 - day 5 - the sunrise over the Tetons was so beautiful, with the clouds hanging over the lake. Then a <u>7 mile hike</u> into them. Loved the <u>horseback ride</u>. Rented a boat in the evening and went for a little ride on the lake. Then drooled on the dock at all the fish that people had caught. It's a shame we're not staying longer - would love to do some fishing. But I'm pretty itchy tonight from plants I rubbed up against on the hike into the Tetons.

Wed - 6/18/80 - day 6 - Yellowstone day trip, to <u>Old Faithful</u>, some <u>Elk</u>, a <u>Moose</u>, swans, rare birds, mule deer, and <u>other scenery and wildlife</u>.

Thurs - 6/19/80 - day 7 - Grand Tetons to Wells, Nevada - took a <u>raft ride</u> down the Snake River, and then headed to Wells, a town of 1,000.

You can link to movies, clips, journal entries, and other rich media on a perspectives Web site.

For example, the companion Web site to this book, at *http://www.papajohn.org*, is being developed in parallel with the book itself. A book can mention punctuating videos with diary extracts and present a rich mixture of text and graphics. Further, it can discuss other multimedia items such as video clips and sound. However, the book is somewhat limited when it comes to illustrating the concepts and examples; the companion Web site doesn't have the same limitations.

Building a rich-media Web site puts the surfer in control of what they want to see, provides what interests them, and delves more deeply into specific topics or perspectives. The example provides individual thoughts of each person, using text and movies, and shows the vacation from each person's perspective. A surfer can browse everyone's view of the vacation, or only one person's.

On the companion Web site, each of the clips used in the vacation memories project appears in multiple places. Video snippets of just a few seconds or longer are integrated into the Web site for the reader to click while they read the text. In the graphic on the previous page, taken from the companion Web site, 15 links are used in just a few paragraphs, with each link being an opportunity for the viewer to see anything from a video snippet to a longer vacation segment to a journal entry.

If you have some space available on a Web server (and just about everyone with an e-mail account has server space available), you might want to explore building a similar site that delivers a rich media experience.

When you import video and when you render your movie, Movie Maker creates a temporary file where it does the conversion and compression or decompression work. This file is created on the hard disk and the directory specified in the General tab on the Options dialog box; see Chapter 4 for more information on these options. When Movie Maker is finished creating the movie, it then writes a copy of the file elsewhere on your computer. The bottom line is that Movie Maker might need roughly twice the free hard disk space as your finished movie will take up. If you're running out of disk space, you might need to delete some files from your computer or move the temporary directory to another hard disk.

Yes, it's easy and fun. But you'll have to learn how to make some appropriate selections when the wizard asks you for them. The options are pretty straightforward and simple to choose when you save your movie.

Ready for Primetime: Saving and Distributing Your Movies

It's finally time to save and distribute some movies. You can burn a couple discs, look at differences in how well they play in various players, and get some feedback from your audience. You can always redo parts if you need to, try something different on your next project, or experiment with each of the following five methods.

Each of the five methods for saving and distributing your movies is easy, quick, and convenient to use. You can save a movie to your hard disk, burn it onto a HighMAT video CD, send it as an e-mail attachment, upload it to your online video hosting service, or transfer it to a tape in your digital camcorder. Each of these methods is as simple as selecting one of the five choices in the main menu and picking a few options. The Save Movie Wizard takes care of most options, with a bit of guidance from you.

With your project file open, start the Save Movie Wizard. Then click File | Save Movie File.

The Save Movie Wizard appears, as shown in Figure 5-1.

Figure 5-1 The Save Movie Wizard lists your five options for your movie file.

You can also start the wizard by going to the Movie Tasks pane and clicking your option. Figure 5-2 shows the Finish Movie options in the Movie Tasks pane.

Each of the options behaves slightly differently, but you'll have no trouble working through them. The following sections present the five options; when you know which movie format you'll use, skip to that section and choose the options appropriate for your finished movie type.

SAVE TO MY COMPUTER

This option saves your movie to your selected folder on the hard disk. The wizard walks you through various pages and offers appropriate options. The first page is

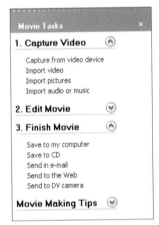

Figure 5-2 The Movie Tasks pane also lists the five options for saving your movie.

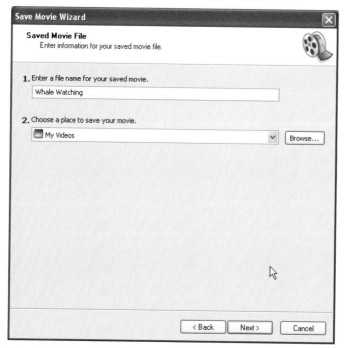

Figure 5-3 The Saved Movie File page lets you type the movie name and choose the location for your movie.

the Saved Movie File page shown in Figure 5-3, where you name your movie and tell Movie Maker 2 where you want it on your hard disk. You can't save over an existing movie; you must either delete the existing movie or use a different name.

The folder that the page shows you at first is the last place to which you saved a movie. The wizard guesses that you'd like to save the new movie there also. If not, browse to and select a different folder. Enter the name for your movie and the file-name and location for your saved movie.

TIP You can use as many as 64 characters for your movie name, so feel free to make it descriptive. The only characters you can't use are these: \ / : * ? " < > |. You don't have to remember which ones are "forbidden" because Movie Maker will tell you if you try to use one to them.

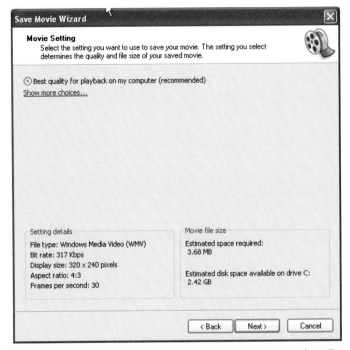

Figure 5-4 The Movie Setting page gives you the option to change the movie quality.

The next page of the wizard is the Movie Setting page shown in Figure 5-4, where you select the quality setting of your movie file. The page is pretty simple, but you make some key choices on it.

When this page first opens, it shows just one option: Best Quality For Playback On My Computer (Recommended). Click the Show More Choices link so it expands the options and looks like Figure 5-5. The Save Movie Wizard provides lots of key information to help you decide the most appropriate choice for your movie.

This is where you get to use your knowledge of quality levels and file sizes. The choice is less tricky than it seems, and the best part is that you'll always have an opportunity to view the finished movie before committing to it. If the quality of the finished movie isn't what you want, you can cancel the wizard and start the saving process again.

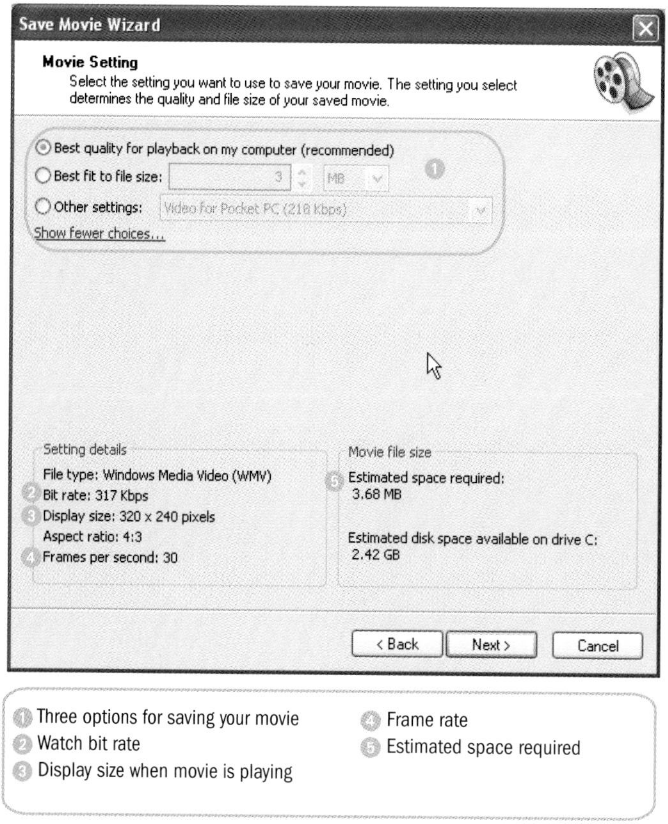

Figure 5-5 The expanded list shows more options for your finished movie.

The three options are as follows:

Best Quality For Playback On My Computer (Recommended) This is a good choice if you're planning to view the movie on your own computer. It's a good all-purpose choice to go with, and it'll be the one you use the most for your first passes at saving a movie. You can then view the finished movie on your computer, and if you don't like it, you can delete the movie or run the wizard again and resave over the existing one. However, if this is the final save of your movie before you burn it to a CD or DVD using another program, you should consider the DV-AVI option in the Other Settings drop-down list.

Best Fit To File Size This choice is a really powerful one. Movie Maker will limit the maximum size of the movie file to the number you select. With it, you can easily control the balance between your file size and quality: the higher the file size, the higher the quality. All you have to do is increment the file size up or down. When you change the final file size, you change the bit rate, display size, and frames per second. This is the best option if you know you have limited disk space or other file size constraints.

> If you use **Best Fit To File Size**, the best selection is by bit rate because you can tailor your movie to the type of connection your viewers are using. Specifically, 300 kilobits per second (Kbps) is a good bit rate for a broadband connection, and 38 Kbps might be too low for a dial-up user with a 56 Kbps modem. Just remember that a low bit rate corresponds to low visual quality, and a high bit rate corresponds to high quality.

Other Settings   This choice provides a drop-down list of options that are often best if you have a specific target audience and, by experience, know the best choice to make. See Figure 5-6 for the list of choices.

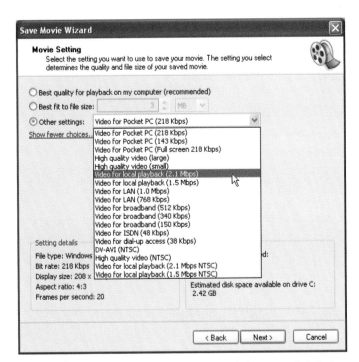

Figure 5-6 The Other Settings list shows the numerous device types and playback speeds you can use for your movie.

These choices give you the ability to tailor your movie to specific playback devices. Each setting makes a distinct difference in the settings and file size information:

Video For Pocket PC   This provides three choices for the different screen sizes of each device type and frame rates per second: 20, 8, and 15.

> **TIP**
>
> The three Pocket PC choices are the only ones in this list that are saved using the older version 7 codecs. All others use the newer version 9 codecs. This is good to know if your audience uses Windows NT or Macintosh computers because their WMV viewers can probably view movies made with the version 7 codecs but might not be able to view version 9 movies. Send them a small test movie made with version 9, and if that doesn't work, try one of the Pocket PC settings instead.

High Quality Video (NTSC)   The large setting makes a movie at 640 × 480 pixels, and the small is at 320 × 240. Both are variable bit rate movies.

Video For Local Playback   This is 640 × 480 pixels with 2.1 megabits per second (Mbps) and 1.5 Mbps.

Video For LAN   This is 1.0 Mbps and 750 Kbps. These are somewhat comparable in quality to the choice of Best Quality For Playback On My Computer (Recommended).

Video For Broadband   There are three choices here, each with a size of 320 × 240 pixels. The 512 and 340 Kbps choices use 30 frames per second, and the lower-rate 150 Kbps uses 15 frames per second. As with the Best Fit To File Size option, to maintain video size and quality, the frame rate is reduced.

> **NOTE**
>
> If you're rendering a group of movies at a particular bit rate, either pay close attention to the pixel size and bit speed or preview the movies after you render them. If one of them is especially short, then the pixel size might jump from 320 × 240 to 640 × 480 so that the movie fits the given bit rate. This makes the movie appear four times larger than the other movies you rendered. If this happens, you might need to render the movie at a lower bit rate to keep the screen sizes equal.

Video For ISDN   This low-bandwidth option results in a small 160 × 120 pixel size at 15 frames per second.

Video For Dial-Up Access   This is another lower-quality option; it results in 160 × 120 pixels at 15 frames per second.

DV-AVI   The bit rate shows as 30 Mbps, even faster than 25 Mbps digital video transfers across Apple FireWire cables. This is the option for the highest-quality file and for the biggest file sizes. Note the dramatic jump in the estimated file size when you select this option.

Video For Local Playback   This is similar to the previous local playback options but with a larger display size of 720 × 480 pixels and fixed bit rates of 2.1 and 1.5 Mbps.

Rather than feeling overwhelmed by the drop-down list, go ahead and select either Best Quality For Playback On My Computer (Recommended) or Best Fit To File Size. Click Next, and your movie will save with the name and file location you gave it earlier.

When you get more experience with how your finished movies look, you can come back and explore the Other Settings list and zero in on the options that'll play back the best for your audience.

SAVE TO CD

Burning movies to CD is a popular choice for movies you create using Movie Maker. CDs are capable of storing approximately 650 megabytes (MB) of data, depending on the settings. Movie Maker 2 includes a technology called HighMAT that dramatically improves the digital media experience on various consumer electronic devices. HighMAT provides a standardized data storage mechanism that improves digital media access technology and increases interoperability between PCs and CD or DVD players.

The quality of HighMAT CDs made by Movie Maker 2, when playing on computers, easily rivals the quality of a DVD, and you can fit about an hour of video on a single CD. If computer-based viewing is for you and you have Windows XP, this is a great option. Playback can be on a computer or a stand-alone DVD player (when available) that supports the HighMAT technology for WMV files.

The HighMAT organization at *http://www.highmat.com* has a free viewer you can download to simulate the experience of playing the CD in a DVD player. The simulation is all that's currently available because the current DVD players with the High-MAT logo don't yet include WMV file support. The viewer runs only on Windows XP. Newer versions of Windows Media Player on computers running versions of Windows other than XP can still play the WMV files on the CD; they just won't have the advantage of the HighMAT menu structure.

To burn movies to a CD, follow these steps:

1. Put a blank or partially filled CD (with previously burned movies from Movie Maker) in your CD burner.

2. Click Save To CD in the Movie Tasks list, or click File | Save Movie File | Save To CD.

3. Type a movie name and a name for your CD, as shown in Figure 5-7. Click Next.

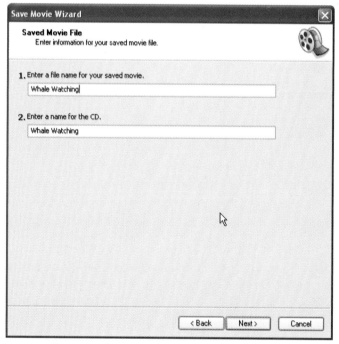

Figure 5-7 Type your movie name and CD name into the Saved Movie File page.

④ Click Best Fit For Recordable CD. Note that you can click Show More Choices to see a page that looks like the one in Figure 5-5. If you click Other Settings, you see a drop-down list like the one in Figure 5-8. Some of the same choices are here as in Figure 5-6, and the various rates change depending on your movie's playback device.

⑤ Click Next.

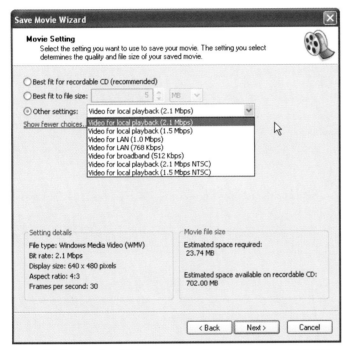

Figure 5-8 The drop-down list gives you more options for burning your movie for a particular playback device.

Movie Maker first renders the movie to a temporary file, copies it onto the CD, and then adds the HighMAT menu structure. If you want to add other movies to the same CD, Movie Maker will automatically do it and update the HighMAT menu structure, continuing to add movies until the CD gets within 50 MB of being full. Movie Maker automatically opens and closes the CD, so you can take a CD that you put a couple movies on a week ago and add another one today.

The HighMAT menu structure uses the first frame of a clip or movie as the thumbnail in the viewer. If your movie starts with a Fade In, From Black effect, then you'll see only a black thumbnail in the menu. Think about adding a still image or clip at the beginning of your movie so that there's something interesting in the menu other than a black square.

SEND IN E-MAIL

Sending a movie as an e-mail attachment should be limited to the smallest movie files and the shortest video clips. This is a great selection if you want to send a very quick, small video—maybe a clip from a movie you're working on—in a low-quality mode. Use it when the message is brief and the content is much more important than the quality. Sometimes a video file with narration, even a short one with poor video quality, can be an extremely effective method of communicating.

The Send In E-Mail option has its limitations. Because the file size must be small to get past most e-mail attachment limits, the movie quality and video size won't be optimal. In addition, people with older computers running Windows 98 or even Windows 95 might have trouble viewing the movie; sometimes, even with broadband connections, the computer just lacks the horsepower needed to play the movie.

Although you could use the wizard to jump right in and render your movie, there's an additional setting you should specify. Follow these steps:

1. Click Tools | Options, and then select the Advanced tab.

2. In the E-Mail section, set the maximum file size. Movie Maker uses this setting to determine the file size, bit rate, and frame rate of your finished movie. If you want acceptable viewing quality and size, figure on about 2 MB per minute of movie; a two-and-a-half-minute movie would be about 5 MB, so you'd set the maximum file size to 5 MB.

3. Return to the Movie Tasks panel.

4. Click Send In E-Mail. Movie Maker immediately renders your movie. When it's done, it'll show you the page in Figure 5-9. You have two options at this

point: play the movie or save a copy of your movie to your hard disk. You can click Next, or you can click one of these two options:

■ If you click Play The Movie, Windows Media Player will load and play the movie, and then it'll return you to the wizard when you close the player. If the movie quality isn't high enough, increase the e-mail file size limit and try again.

■ If you click Save A Copy Of My Movie On My Computer, the Save Movie dialog box appears. You can give your movie a filename and select the folder for it; by default, the folder is the My Videos folder. You'll have a copy attached to your sent e-mail message, so you might not need to do this.

⑤ The wizard creates a new e-mail message in your default e-mail software, fills in the subject line with the name of the movie project, and attaches a copy of the movie to the message. Note the file size of the attachment; if you have any last thoughts about the size of the movie and your audience's capabilities, now is the time to correct this (usually making the movie smaller). Address it, add your comments, and click Send.

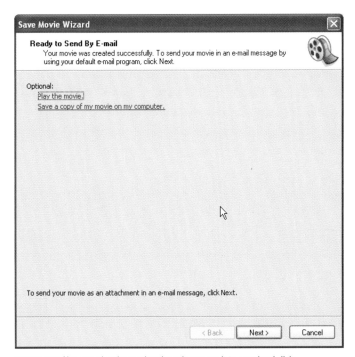

Figure 5-9 You can play the rendered movie or save it to your hard disk.

E-mail attachments are always WMV files created with the version 9 codecs. If your recipients will be viewing the attachment on Macintosh or Windows NT systems, you might need to choose a different format. Earlier versions of WMV cannot read the version 9 codecs, and you must download the codec package in order to play movies. See the Appendix for details on updating the codecs.

SEND TO THE WEB

Saving a movie to the Web is particularly helpful when you use an online video hosting service. The hosting service provides the hardware for you to store and make your movies available, and it provides plenty of bandwidth for your friends and family to view the movies over the Internet. This makes it handy when you don't want the headache or network administration hassles of running your own video server out of your office, basement, or spare bedroom. If you have an account with such a service, this choice lets you automatically link to your account and save your movie to their servers. Follow these steps:

1. Click Save To Web in the Movie Tasks pane, or click File | Save Movie File | The Web.

2. Enter the filename for the movie, and click Next.

3. The wizard provides a different set of choices than when you saved the movie to your computer. Figure 5-10 shows the list expanded with all the choices. You have three choices for speed and quality:

   Dial Up Modem (56 Kbps)   160 × 120 pixels, 15 frames per second, 38 Kbps

   ISDN (64 Kbps)   160 × 120 pixels, 15 fps, 48 Kbps

   DSL, Cable Modem, or Higher (384 Kbps)   320 × 240 pixels, 30 frames per second, 340 Kbps

   Note you can still select options based on file size and playback device. See the "Save to My Computer" section for a discussion of these other options.

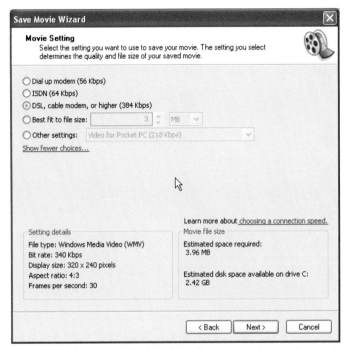

Figure 5-10 Select your movie's playback based on your viewer's connection speed.

④ Click Next. The next step renders the temporary movie file and then asks you to select from your pick list of online host services, as shown in Figure 5-11. The wizard also offers a link to sign up with a provider if you don't have one.

⑤ If you select the Sign Up Now link for a host provider, your Internet browser will open to a Microsoft page with currently affiliated providers. You can expect to see more of these services as more people use Movie Maker 2 and the demand for such services picks up.

⑥ By clicking the Next button of the wizard, a copy of the movie is sent to the provider, and you're given options for saving a copy on your computer and for viewing it on the provider's Web site after the wizard finishes.

⑦ The link to saving a copy on your computer asks you to name the movie file and select a location.

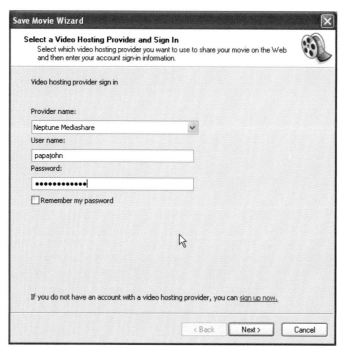

Figure 5-11 Enter your provider name, user name, and password for your video hosting account.

⑧ If you use the check box to watch it on the Web site when finished, you'll be connected to the online host to view the movie and to manage your online movie library.

SEND TO DV CAMERA

This option sends the movie to a tape in your digital camcorder. The option to save your movie back to a digital video camera is an appealing option for several reasons:

- Digital video cameras record your movie in the highest-available quality, DV-AVI, which gives you the greatest flexibility for any future work you might want to do with the movie.

- DV cameras make for more flexible offline, long-term storage of your movies and clips.

- You can play back your movie on any TV, without needing any special equipment such as a DVD player.

- You can copy your movie to VCR tapes—which is helpful when distant relatives don't have the latest and greatest computer or video technology for viewing your movie over the Internet or on a DVD player.

Before you save your movie back to a camcorder, you'll need to make sure it's connected, turned on, and ready to record your movie. Follow these steps:

1. Turn on the camera while it's connected to an external power source. This ensures the battery doesn't run down during the rendering and transfer process.

2. Connect the computer and camcorder with a FireWire cable.

3. Turn the camcorder switch to the VTR or VCR mode (not the Play mode). A Windows pop-up dialog box will appear with a list of applications to use. Choose the option Take No Action.

4. Click Send To DV Camera in the Movie Tasks pane, or click File | Save Movie File | DV Camera.

5. Use the camcorder controls to go to the point on the tape that you want to start the recording, as shown in Figure 5-12. A digital 8 or mini-digital camcorder is limited to a one-hour video.

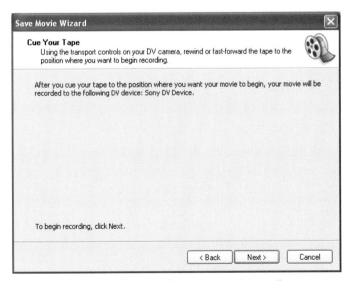

Figure 5-12 Cue the recorder tape to where you want to start recording.

6 Click Next. You'll get the warning that the content will be overwritten.

7 The progress dialog box shows you the percentage saved and the estimated time remaining, as shown in Figure 5-13.

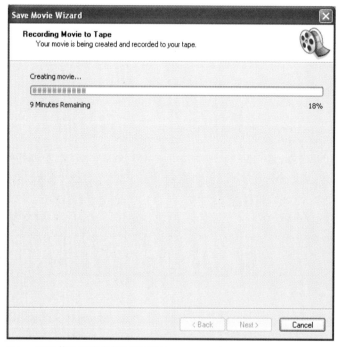

Figure 5-13 Your movie is being saved to your camcorder.

Rendering and exporting a movie back to a digital camcorder is demanding for your computer. If you notice glitches in the video or audio during the transfer, assume those glitches will be transferred as well. Stop the transfer, and tune up your computer before trying again. See the Appendix for details on improving performance and defragmenting your hard disk.

If all goes well from the Movie Maker perspective, the wizard will reach the end of the progress meter and tell you that your movie was successfully recorded on the tape in your DV camera.

Even if you were monitoring the process on your camera, it's time to watch it again to verify that it plays smoothly. If you watched it closely during the transfer process, then spot-check it to confirm the process worked. You can play it back on the camcorder, or you can hook your camcorder up to a TV and play it there—a big help in spotting small flaws that might have crept in during the rendering process. The amount of checking that you do should be consistent with the importance of the tape.

Learning About Burning DVDs

Most people today say, "I want to burn my movies to a DVD." The DVD revolution has swept through the electronics realm, making professional-quality home movies possible. While DVD players and DVD movies surged in popularity, people began asking for DVD burners for computers; CD burners were no longer sufficient. Manufacturers responded: prices on DVD burners have dropped, and reliability has increased. Many computers now ship with DVD burners that can turn home computers into robust movie-making machines. This technology was unimaginable ten years ago; today it's a reality.

Because there are a number of hardware-dependent DVD standards that are closely tied to specific DVD burners, Movie Maker doesn't currently support saving a movie directly to DVD. Instead, it's a two-step process: you must save it to disk in a format that can be used by a third-party program and then use that program to burn your movies onto a DVD. Then your movies can be viewed on a TV while they're played on standard DVD players.

Other programs use a similar method for burning DVDs. If you have one of these programs, these are the basic steps to follow:

1. Save your movies in a format that your DVD burning software can use. Check the instructions or the online help file to see if there are any specific format requirements, such as bit rate or screen size, that you need for your movies before you burn them to DVD. In general, you want the highest-quality movies available for the burning software.

DVDS DON'T ALWAYS PLAY WELL TOGETHER

Before you rush out to buy a DVD burner or start using the one you already have, you should know that there are various DVD formats on the market. The most common are DVD-R and DVD+R and their siblings DVD-RW and DVD+RW. The "minus" formats are related, as are the "plus" formats. Although manufacturers have tried to make the different formats compatible, DVD burners for one format might not write to the other formats, and some early model DVD players might not read incompatible formats. The issue is most common when moving a disc between computers with different DVD drives or between a computer and a DVD player. For the most part, you shouldn't have any problems. However, if you have compatibility concerns, take a look at the documentation for your burner and DVD player to see which formats are supported; you want the DVD burner and DVD player to support the same "flavor" of DVD recording. If the documentation isn't clear, or if you've misplaced the documents, you can always burn a test disc with a short movie on it and then test it on the other device to see if the systems are compatible.

There are also other disc formats available. Video Compact Discs (VCDs) and Super Video Compact Discs (SVCDs) also play in DVD players. VCDs use MPEG-1 files, which are lower in quality than the MPEG-2 files used for SVCDs and DVDs. Although there's nothing inherently wrong with these other formats, the primary advantage of DVD over VCD is that it can store more data. So if you have the option, use SVCDs or DVDs.

2 Select the main window and background. When you first put a DVD into a player, you're taken to a menu that provides you with a graphical list of movies and lets you select movies or other submenus. This step lets you put a framework in place for your movies. You can always come back and edit or change the background or the look and feel of this screen.

3 Add your movies. Depending on the software and the main window you chose in step 1, there are slots for you to add your movies. You can usually add or edit titles, descriptions, and other visual details that help your viewers figure out which movie to select. Some DVD burning software automatically creates thumbnails for the menu; others run a loop of the first few seconds of the movie. (This is a good reason for having a short credit screen at the start of your movies!)

4 Make any final adjustments or edits. Rearrange the videos, change backgrounds, and do whatever you want to get the right look and feel for your DVD.

5 Burn it! The DVD rendering and burning process will take quite a bit of time. DVDs hold up to 4.7 gigabytes (GB) of data, and if you have a full disc, your computer will be working overtime for quite a while. Like with the rendering process in Movie Maker, you need enough room on your hard disk for temporary file storage. Make sure you have the room available.

When the process is complete, you'll have a DVD that you can take to the player, hook up to your TV, and play back for your friends and family. You should probably preview it on your computer first just to make sure everything looks and works well.

There are several software programs you can use to burn movies to DVD. You might have received one that was bundled with your computer or DVD burner, or you might have picked one up from the Internet or from your local software store. Each has its strong points, and you should look at various packages to see if they have the features you want and to see if the program feels right and works easily for you. What works for your kids might be too flashy for your style, so surf over to the manufacturer's Web sites to see some screenshots or to see demos in action. There's bound to be at least one program that looks and feels right and that matches the way you work.

BURN YOUR OWN DVDS
QUICKLY AND EASILY

The DVD burning process is pretty straightforward, without a lot of effort needed on your part. Nearly all software packages give you the ability to express your creativity in the movies you make by letting you edit the menus, backgrounds, and other details. As an example, the following is the DVD burning process using MyDVD 4.5 by Sonic Solutions. The newer versions of MyDVD can use either WMV files or DV-AVI files from Movie Maker 2 for creating DVDs. This is a great option, especially with DV-AVI; although the files are bigger, you'll get the highest-quality movie by creating your movies using DV-AVI and then importing them into your DVD burning software. Follow these steps:

1. Start MyDVD. The following graphic shows the MyDVD welcoming screen. Click the first menu choice to start your first DVD project.

This is the opening screen you see when you start MyDVD.

② Click the generic title text that the new project has. Click the title to edit it. Your new project opens using the NatureMotion style, complete with fluffy white clouds. There are two other styles available from the Edit Style button in the main icon bar under the drop-down menu; explore all three, and select the one you want for the DVD project. Each of the styles has different visual and audio themes.

③ Use the Get Movies icon at the left to open your My Videos folder and drill down to your movies. You can select more than one at a time and open them to add thumbnails to the page. There's a limit of six movies on a page. The following graphic shows the main working window of MyDVD after adding a few movie files, changing the generic main title, and opting to see the TV-safe viewing area—the dotted outline.

A backdrop has been chosen and movies added to the first project.

④ If you have more than six movies you want to put on your DVD, consider creating submenus that have similar topics or groupings for your movies (by date or time, by theme, or by people). You can add submenus by clicking the Add Submenu icon and then adding movies to each submenu. MyDVD automatically generates navigation buttons to move between the different menus.

⑤ While you add movies, watch the statistics at the lower left of the working window. The DVD starts with 4.7 GB of space, and the figure under it shows the remaining space based on the movies you've already placed into the project. Another indication of space is the bright-red Burn button. It'll turn grayish if you get to the point of having too many movies to fit on your DVD. It'll stay that way until you drop enough from the project to go back below the DVD size constraint.

⑥ Once you're happy with the way your menus and animations look, you're ready to put a blank DVD in and burn it. Save the DVD project, and click the red button when you're ready. If you have a full DVD, the process takes several hours, depending on your DVD burner's speed and computer's horsepower. With the example project shown in this sidebar, the whole process took almost three hours—about two hours to render the MPEG-2 and other files needed for the DVD and then an hour to do the burning. If you want to make multiple copies, MyDVD offers the ability to create multiple DVDs, which saves the two-hour rendering time for subsequent copies.

There's one key point to keep in mind: when you're working in MyDVD, you can render animations that are applied to the DVD. The animations include the clouds moving when the DVD menu is open, and each of the six thumbnails of the movies on the page or submenu will be cycling through the first 15 seconds of their video tracks. The thumbnails play the video content only while music consistent with the style of the DVD plays in the background. Click the smaller rectangular button with the little runner on it, just to the lower right of the Preview button, to add the animations. Nice effects!

You might want to visit some of these sites:

Easy CD & DVD Creator by Roxio   Using this program, you can make CDs and DVDs on your own computer using your own DVD burner. You can also make copies of data, music, and movies for backups or for viewing on your DVD player. Learn more about the software and other products at *http://www.roxio.com*.

MyDVD and DVDit! by Sonic Solutions   MyDVD and DVDit! are two of several products related to data mastering, backing up, and editing made by Sonic. You can learn more about MyDVD at *http://www.mydvd.com* and about DVDit! at *http://www.dvdit.com*.

Nero by Ahead Software   Nero lets you burn CDs and DVDs for your own movies, for data backup, and for still images or audio. You can download the software at *http://www.nero.com*.

Ulead DVD MovieFactory by Ulead   DVD MovieFactory lets you create CDs and DVDs with various menu systems and create backups or copies for friends. You can find out more information and download trial software at *http://www.ulead.com*.

Glossary

Kbps — The acronym for "kilobits per second." This is a measurement used for calculating data speeds. It's most often used for Digital Subscriber Lines (DSL), cable modems, and dial-up modems.

Mbps — The acronym for "megabits per second." This is a measurement used for calculating data speeds, most commonly over local area networks or the Internet.

HighMAT — The acronym for "High-Performance Media Access Technology." This is a standardized data storage technology codeveloped by Microsoft and Matsushita (Panasonic) that improves digital media access and increases interoperability between devices such as PCs and CD or DVD players.

WMV — The acronym for "Windows Media Video." This is a specific codec that's used in both Movie Maker and Windows Media Player for recording and playing back digital video and audio.

PART II

Making movies is only the beginning. Using Windows Movie Maker 2 and a little creativity, you can take your movies in new and exciting directions. Give your family a hand at creating their own version of your last family vacation. Put together a visual and aural history of your relatives for your very own genealogy project. Get wacky and make movie trailers for movies *you'd* like to see. And, if you're interested in taking your skills to the next level, you can learn more about movie-making hardware and software and even how to set up and direct your own project from start to finish.

Exploring the Fun Zone

- **Assemble Your Family Treasures from the Past**

- **Take Pictures and Video to Use in Your Movie**

- **Publish the Movie and Give It a Prominent Position as a New Family Treasure**

Create Your Own Living History

CHAPTER 6

We all have relatives, and most of us at times become interested in exploring a bit about who they are and where they came from. For some, genealogy is a minor passing interest; for others, it's a consuming passion. When you combine the power of the Internet for information gathering, your own storytelling ability and tales, and the multimedia tools that are available to you, you can build movies that let you and generations to come experience your family history. You can be the catalyst to pull it all together, adding new multimedia dimensions of sound and video to those older ones of fading pictures and letters and notes. What's great about such a project is that it can never begin too early or too late, and it never has to be finished—you can just pass it along to others for additions.

A glance at a photo might prompt a memory that your great-grandmother was a schoolteacher who taught music to students in her parlor.

Coming Attractions

Go to your attic or basement, and open some old boxes of family treasures. Take pictures and video, and scan the items. If you come across a marked-up music or song score, find a copy of the music to punctuate the audio of your living history project. Your collections of treasures have waited a long time for this moment. Today you have the right tools to do it—make documentary movies that you and your family for generations to come will enjoy, treasure, and pass along.

The living history project turns you into a detective, a research historian, and a filmmaker using your computer, your family, and any pictures or documents they might have collected over the years. With Movie Maker 2, you can blend these together in ways that weren't possible using only paper charts or family tree software. You can create a living document that shows aspects of your family that were previously forgotten or highlight specific events that had a lasting effect on your family's history. And you don't have to create only one movie; you can use this as the foundation for a series of short clips or films that record who you are and where you came from. The best part? You can always add more information when you discover it because it's as easy as dragging, dropping, and rendering a movie. So, get ready to tell your family's story, complete with pictures, clips, and documents! This chapter takes you through the steps to create your own living history.

Step 1: Select a Topic

If you've worked on genealogy projects before, you know they can quickly expand in scope, stretching back in time and across families and countries. Direct descendants, lineal ancestors, and third, fourth, and fifth cousins—a tree can develop many branches, each with its own fascinating story to tell. Part of the fun of genealogy is the stories you hear and the facts you learn about your family and your ancestors. With this Movie Maker living history project, the problem isn't thinking up a theme or topic; it's how to limit the story you want to tell in a particular movie. A thorough discussion of how to conduct genealogy research is beyond the scope of this book, but the following project ideas can get you started:

Coming to America   Many people have relatives who came to America in the late 1800s or early 1900s. Fortunately, there are lots of records available from that time period, including photographs and immigration documents. Some of your living relatives might be able to tell stories of when they came over with their parents or can relate what they heard from their own parents or great-grandparents. From these reminiscences, you can build a movie that documents their immigration and arrival. The example in this chapter shows how you can construct a similar movie using this theme. The focus is on the girl standing on the chair in Figure 6-1.

Figure 6-1 Everyone's family has a story that's waiting to be told.

A Day in the Life   This example takes a closer look at one particular relative or ancestor, mixing pictures of him or her with pictures, movies, or newspaper clippings dealing with the daily life and events that were important during his or her life. Many people's families were involved with farming or agriculture; others were getting started in factories, working hard at blue-collar jobs so their children could go to college. Still others made a living in the big city, working in a mom-and-pop store in an ethnic neighborhood. All these environments are fertile grounds for a movie and can help give the family story a larger context.

A Tale from the Past   Many people have family stories that have been handed down through the years. Some stories are recent, and others go back for decades or generations. You might be able to act out the story using other members of the family. Or, if it was one that made headlines, you might have a great source of pictures and clippings you can use as a resource. In other cases, just having a relative narrate the story for the camera and interspersing it with pictures or illustrations you find from your family archives or on the Web might be more than enough to preserve the story for future generations.

Branches on the Family Tree   It's easy to get carried away with this topic; once you start researching, it's hard to stop, especially when you find new branches or information about ancestors. In this example, you portray in movie format the information you'd find in a paper drawing of the tree: photographs of people, paintings, birth or marriage certificates, death certificates, or gravestone rubbings—anything that ties the lineal descendants together. This is a more involved exercise than the other three because you'll want to include some kind of visual family tree to help give your viewers a reference point. But it's one of the most rewarding films you can make, and it might inspire you to make other movies about specific ancestors.

These topics are good ones to get you started. While you explore your family and its roots, other ideas will pop up. Write them down, and come back to them when you want new additions to your genealogy portfolio. Genealogy is one of those areas that, if you do a good job with these movies, can turn into a semiprofessional hobby where you make films for other people who lack the time or skills to do it themselves.

Step 2: Round Up the Source Files

You can find genealogy source files in every family, and depending on the project, you can find other source materials that can be used within the movie. Don't let the following list scare you. It's not meant to be a list of all the places you *must* search for information; it's a list of places you *can* look if you're drawing a blank about where to go. Remember that the Internet provides you with instant access to many of these resources—there are Web sites dedicated to genealogy research, companies that sell software that helps you organize your family tree and related information, and databases of census statistics that can be used in your quest. Dip into the sources that intrigue you, and leave the rest for later or another movie project. The goal is to have fun finding out about your own family!

FINDING THE SOURCE MATERIALS

In general, you can categorize the research materials as primary and secondary sources. Primary sources are ones you can get information about your relatives "first hand." They deal with specifics and give you the core information you need to help you tell your story about their lives. Primary sources include the following:

- All living relatives

- Close family friends or neighbors

- Any existing film footage of your family members (Super-8, VHS, or even older film or video footage that has family members in it)

- Family photographs, picture albums, portraits or paintings of people

- Any audio recordings of family members that capture their stories or even just their voices during family events (old cassette tapes, radio interviews, even old record albums)

- Life event records (as known as "vital statistics"): birth certificates, marriage certificates, baptismal records, diplomas, death certificates, census data, immigration records

- Diaries, journals, letters, family Bibles, baby books

- Other genealogists who have done research on your family tree

HANDLE WITH CARE!

If you have a list of source materials and you're starting to collect them for your project, remember that you need to take care with the materials. Many of them aren't archival quality, so they get fragile and brittle with age. Other materials might feel robust but are sensitive to bright lights such as those you might find on a scanner. The following are some guidelines you can follow when assembling your source materials.

OLD PHOTOGRAPHS

If you want to use old family photographs, you might not be able to remove them from a frame or scrapbook without damaging them. If this happens, you can either take a "picture of the picture" (preferred) or scan the image into your computer. Set up a still camera or your digital camcorder on a tripod, adjust the lighting in the room so that no reflections are cast from any glass in the frame or cellophane protectors in the scrapbook, and snap an image or run a few seconds of film. Try several different exposure and light levels, as well as distances and focus adjustments for the picture. This will give you a range of images for your project, so you can select the best one.

The graphic below, showing a mixture of old and new photos, is perfect for getting some digital images. In the graphic on the following page, the girl who was shown standing on the chair in Figure 6-1 is sitting in a chair holding a doll.

Almost everyone has a table full of family pictures such as this one.

Let's focus on her picture and get a source picture from it for the sample movie. She was a young girl in New York City, a few years after emigrating from Italy.

Should you use a still camera or camcorder? Should you remove the picture from the frame and scan it, or should you scan it while in the frame? A camcorder, using natural light, is the least intrusive method. The image might not be sufficient for high-quality digital photo work, but it'll be perfect for using in a movie. And you can take the video without having to touch the table or picture.

Mount the camcorder on a tripod and zoom into the picture. You can zoom pretty far and still stay within the optical range of the camcorder lens. The one being used, shown in the following graphic, has an 18× optical zoom feature. With good low-light capabilities, you can easily shoot some great clips while avoiding reflections off the glass.

The star of the movie

Our star, through the eyes of the camcorder

The following graphic shows the overall arrangement of the camcorder and the table. What you see in the LCD screen or viewfinder is what you'll have on your computer and in your movie. The camcorder screens that flip out are handy for previewing the video while taking it.

Setting up the table and camcorder

You can sometimes scan photographs without damaging them. If you use care, you can put the entire picture or scrapbook page on the scanner bed and scan the photograph or item of interest. If you have doubts about whether to scan a photo, especially an old one, take a picture instead. If you want, you can take the photo to a photo lab or camera store and have them convert the photo to a digital image. They have more sophisticated equipment and can deliver high-quality images without damaging the original.

Secondary sources are ones that are still connected to the relative in some way but aren't necessarily directly related to the relatives or the story. These include the following:

- Property, real estate, or mortgage records

- Newspaper clippings, magazines, or books

- Yearbooks or annuals

- Wills, trusts, or deeds

- Paychecks or pay stubs

- Community achievement awards

- Membership in clubs, organizations, groups, or sports associations

- Awards or honors

- Souvenirs, relics, or heirlooms

These sources can often lead to information that isn't otherwise available or lead you to primary sources you haven't uncovered yet.

Depending on the story you want to tell and how much detail you want to add, there are other background sources you can include as part of your research pattern:

- Old movies and film footage of generic subjects

- Pictures of towns, homes, factories, railroads, and ships

- Information about specific time periods or towns and cities

- Newspapers or pictures of notable events, people, and places

- Information on churches, buildings, and transportation methods

- Books or biographies of people and events

- Anything that adds life, color, background, and dimension to the story

The most important sources are people. They're the best source you can go to for information about relatives, events, places, and other people. If you can get them to narrate a story on film, that's outstanding! You can also use any of the other materials listed in this chapter as ticklers to help them remember details that otherwise might be lost in the mists of time. Handing over a photograph of ancestors and asking about them is one of the easiest ways to get information about the people in your history. A glance at a photo might prompt a memory that your great grandmother was a school-teacher who taught music to students in her parlor. That kind of detail is invaluable in rounding out the character and feel of places and people in your background.

The second most valuable sources are the documentary evidence that people leave behind, such as vital statistics. You need to turn to these documents when you don't have living relatives who can provide information for you.

NEWSPAPERS, CLIPPINGS, BOOKS, AND MAGAZINE ARTICLES

Images of the originals are almost always more compelling than electronic text downloaded from the Internet. You can make copies of older documents at libraries or sometimes from the original printer, such as a newspaper that's still in business. Scanning these documents can be an iffy proposition, though; many older documents are sensitive to bright lights and become more brittle with exposure to photocopiers, scanners, and other imaging devices. If these sources are at libraries, explain how you'll use the document and ask about the best way to make a copy. They might have equipment that can make copies that don't damage the originals. And most will allow nonflash photography, again perfect for a camcorder with low-light capability.

Remember that it's better to take a picture (no flash!) of the document in low light with a longer exposure time than it is to brightly light it.

OTHER PEOPLE'S STUFF

If you're using images of homes, heirlooms, or furniture, make sure you obtain permission first and you handle the items with the greatest care. If people are kind enough to let you into their homes to take pictures of where your ancestors once lived, remember that you're a guest. Also, they might be able to offer more information about your ancestors, the house, the town, or common events in the neighborhood that can open up new avenues to explore.

If you're doing headstone or gravestone rubbings, check with the caretaker. Some stones require special care or materials; others might be "off limits" to physical contact with anything other than rain and wind. Camcorder or digital camera pictures of such objects are even easier than a rubbing.

SOURCES ON THE INTERNET

The Internet is a great source of information for your research. Digitized images, films, articles, period music, other people's research, and background information are available for a quick download. The big caution here is copyright violation. You might not be able to use some images and movies unless you pay a licensing fee; others are free, but you must give credit. Without going into details about copyright law and fair use exceptions, make it a habit to inquire about copyright if you're using someone else's original work.

BUILDING YOUR PROJECT

The example in this chapter assembles information from a number of different sources. The subject is my mother-in-law, who came to America from Italy in 1920. She, like many in her generation, entered through Ellis Island in New York City and ended up living much of her life in that city. The short film being made for the example focuses on her trip to America, giving viewers an impression of the sights and sounds of her journey.

To start with, I'll use some still pictures of her and her family. A natural place to start searching for information about her is the Ellis Island Foundation Web site (*http://www.ellisislandrecords.org*), where all their immigration records are available. The records, including Figure 6-2, show she sailed from Italy on the *Lafayette*, which arrived in New York City on October 18, 1920. The passenger manifest lists her mother. Her father had immigrated earlier.

Name:	Colpo, Teresa
Ethnicity:	Italian
Place of Residence:	P. Vicenza, Italy
Date of Arrival:	18 Oct 1920
Age on Arrival:	29y
Gender:	F
Marital Status:	M
Ship of Travel:	Lafayette
Port of Departure:	Le Havre, Seine-Inferior, France

Figure 6-2 The Internet is a powerful tool for conducting genealogy research.

The online information includes images of the passenger manifest, details of the *Lafayette*, including pictures of the ship, and ideas about New York City circa 1920, as shown in Figure 6-3.

Lafayette

Associated Passenger	Date of Arrival	Port of Departure	Line #	Page #	120
Colpo, Teresa	October 18, 1920	Le Havre	0017	previous	next

Manifest for Lafayette
Sailing from Le Havre

Name	Gender	Age	Married	Ethnicity	Place of Residence
0001.Accassato, Francesco	M	28y	S	Italian	Caserta, S Italy
0002.Camerota, Maria	F	33y	M	Italian	Nettuno, Italy
0003.Camerota, Romilia	F	9y	S	Italian	Nettuno, Italy
0004.Camerota, Jole	F	6y	S	Italian	Nettuno, Italy
0005.Camerota, Matia	F	3y	S	Italian	Nettuno, Italy
0006.Camerota, Pasqualino	M	2y	S	Italian	Nettuno, Italy
0007.Camerota, Anna	F	8m	S	Italian	Nettuno, Italy
0008.Cumpanelli, Giuseppe	M	17y	S	Italian	Loreto, Italy
0009.Carrone, Giorgio	M	60y	M	Italian	Loreto, Italy
0010.Cattella, Domenico	M	57y	M	Italian	Canneto, Italy
0011.Callini, Giudo	M	27y	M	Italian	Ciro, Italy
0012.Cantelo, Cabriele	M	25y	S	Italian	Lusiana, Italy
0013.Corradin, Caterina	F	30y	S	Italian	Lusiana, Italy
0014.Carnovale, Vincenzo	M	20y	S	Italian	Cantonia, Italy
0015.Canaglia, Francesco	M	27y	S	Italian	Lusiana, Italy
0016.Colasacco, Emensto	M	32y	M	Italian	Capestrano, Italy
0017.Colpo, Teresa	F	29y	M	Italian	P. Vicenza, Italy
0018.Colpo, Fortunata	F	4y	S	Italian	P. Vicenza, Italy
0019.Colpo, Jean	M	2y	S	Italian	P. Vicenza, Italy
0020.Crivelli, Filippo	M	20y	S	Italian	Eufrenia, Italy
0021.Coletta, Lucia	F	16y	S	Italian	Civitaquana, Italy
0022.Colo, Vincenzo	M	22y	S	Italian	S. Severo, Italy
0023.Di Vecchia, Bartolomea	M	21y	S	Italian	S. Eufrenia, Italy
0024.D'Amico, Annina	F	32y	S	Italian	Chieti, Italy
0025.Donatelli, Giovanni	M	60y	M	Italian	Lattomanapello, Italy
0026.D'Emilio, Angelo	M	29y	S	Italian	Pio Camere, Italy
0027.De Palma, Tomaso	M	27y	M	Italian	Bitanto, Italy
0028.Di Francesco, Antonietta	F	32y	M	Italian	Montrazzolo, Italy
0029.Di Francesco, Angelo	M	9y	S	Italian	Montrazzolo, Italy
0030.Di Nizio, Galizio	M	30y	M	Italian	Montrazzolo, Italy

Associated Passenger	Date of Birth	Port of Departure	Line #	Page #	120
Colpo, Teresa	October 18, 1920	Le Havre	0017	previous	next

Figure 6-3 Passenger manifests are fantastic springboards for finding more information about families.

Some background research provides footage of New York City from a short documentary film about the Third Avenue elevated train in New York City, which was produced in the 1950s. Many archival videos such as this one are available for download from the Internet Archive Web site (*http://www.archive.org*), which provides a collection of older material that has passed its copyright time. The short video clip would give some older New York City flavor by showing an elevated train with the Empire State Building in the background.

> **NOTE** The Third Avenue elevated train was built in the 1870s, so that fits with the overall time period of 1920. But the Empire State Building, which gives such a strong mental image of New York City, wasn't finished until 1931. If you're striving for historical authenticity, you can use footage that doesn't include the building. But, for this chapter's example, you can be a bit more liberal in using whatever fits in the theme.

Finally, for background audio, there are segments of the old movie about the elevated train that have music and nice, older city ambient sounds. Along with some personal documents, the source materials are complete and ready to be imported into Movie Maker.

Step 3: Import the Source Material

If you followed the steps in Chapter 1 and read about creating additional effects in Chapter 2, you have the basic tools you need to bring the materials into Movie Maker and start constructing your project. For the example in this chapter, there are two video clips, four old pictures that were scanned to create digital images, three downloaded images from the Ellis Island Foundation Web site, and two standard introduction and closing clips that are attached to every project. The project's audio was included in the downloaded video file, so no additional audio sources were needed.

I created a new collection for the source files for this project, with the Genealogy collection located under the existing Current Projects collection. Figure 6-4 shows the Genealogy collection after the source files were imported and consolidated into it.

I imported the still images all at once to the collection by selecting them in the file browser and dragging and dropping them into the contents pane.

The video files I downloaded from the Internet Archive Web site presented a challenge. The archive Web site offers two versions of each file for downloading. One is an MPEG-2 file, and the other an AVI file encoded with the DivX codec. These formats sometimes offer challenges when using them as source files in Movie Maker. My usual choice is to download the AVI/DivX files because they oftentimes offer the best blend of quality, file size, and ease of use in Movie Maker 2, provided the needed DivX codec is obtained and used.

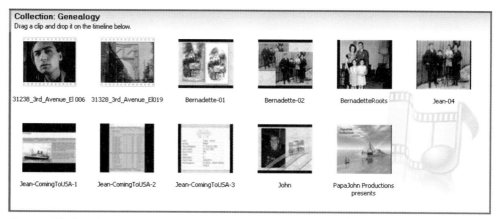

Figure 6-4 The Genealogy collection holds copies of all the files needed to assemble the project.

> **TIP** Sometimes video files that are encoded with MPEG-2 or DivX codecs are involved in "hiccups" during project previewing or rendering. I'll often take a video that was downloaded from the Internet Archive Web site and use Movie Maker to create a WMV or DV-AVI file from it. Then I use that new file as the source file for project editing.

Step 4: Review Your Clips in the Collection

With all the clips in your collection, it's time to take a good look at each. This is the time when you can split source clips into two or more smaller ones so you have only the necessary source files in your collection. For example, if you're downloading a large file from the Internet Archive Web site, you might only want to use parts of the documentary for your movie. Follow the instructions on splitting clips so that you capture only the parts you want—in this case, a shot of the elevated train was needed, so it made sense to make a separate clip out of that part of the source footage.

After importing your files, you might have some that don't quite fill the screen. Movie Maker 2 maintains image proportions when a picture doesn't fit quite right into the 4:3 ratio that's the norm for video in North America. This results in "black bars" either at the top and bottom of the image, much like a widescreen movie that plays on a standard TV, or at the sides of the image. Some people prefer not having any black space; for them, it's time to go to a picture editing application and crop the pictures to fit the ratio. For this movie, wanting it to look old, the black spaces aren't a problem and don't detract from the story. You can try building a movie without cropping and editing your images and see how it comes out; you can always go back and make edits later.

Step 5: Make a Great Introduction

The exercise in Chapter 1 showed you how to create an introduction: a still image that captures the theme, a text overlay, and a video clip or two. You can add all this to your living history project to add emphasis to the story you're trying to tell. If you have a standard introduction that you use for your movie projects, you can use that as a leader into the main movie. If not, you can use an image from a film clip or a still image that you hold on the screen for several seconds with a text overlay explaining the topic of the film.

This chapter's example starts with the standard introduction that's used for many of the book's sample movies. Despite spending a lot of time doing research, there weren't many old pictures available for use for the entire video, so starting with the standard logo was the best option. The opening clip is followed by an old picture of my mother-in-law's mother and her grandmother so that two generations of relatives are shown. This helps tie the movie together for the descendants, giving a visual reference of those who came before my mother-in-law. Following the still image is the first text effect, a simple title that aligns with the simplistic titling you see in movies from the 1920s.

Because the movie is attempting to portray a Coming to America theme from the 1920s, some transitions and effects make the movie look contemporaneous with film footage from that time. The introduction starts with a Fade In, From Black effect. Then a couple more special effects make the film look older. The two most useful ones are the Film Age, Oldest effect to make the movies look older, and the Grayscale effect to make all the footage look like black-and-white footage from that era.

After this work on the introduction, the movie consists of three clips lasting nine-and-a-quarter seconds. This is a reminder that great introductions don't need to be long, involved, or fancy; you just need to hook the viewer's interest and give them a sense of what they'll be seeing.

Step 6: Add Clips to the Body

The body is where you get into the fun part of telling your relative's story. Just as in Chapter 1, you drag and drop clips, images, and audio files in the storyboard and time-line, trim clips, and move elements around until the story flows and feels right. This is also where you can indulge your creativity, adding details that might have come to light during your research phase. Figure 6-5 shows the clips that form the body.

Figure 6-5 The storyboard is a great place for viewing all your clips and images at one time.

You can add various clips, images, and effects during the "fun phase" of movie mak-ing. For this example, I added clips from the Ellis Island archives to the storyboard, showing the boat, the passenger manifest, and my mother-in-law's personal document. I added a text effect announcing her arrival date in New York City, along with the only picture in the set that showed the three people who had made the trip. The picture is repeated so that different effects can be used; this is a nice way to add dynamic feel-ing to still images and help your viewers focus on different aspects of the same docu-ment or image. The final clip in the body is the elevated train in New York City, with the Empire State Building in the background. The video clip anchors the city setting.

I added audio in the Timeline view, using the audio from the archive movie. The audio used a fade in at the beginning and a fade out at the end, a nice touch to add when you use a segment of an audio track that's part of a longer audio clip.

As for effects, the old pictures and archive footage didn't need effects added to them because they already had the aged look from the simple passage of time.

Step 7: Add the Ending

Your ending can be any clip or image that helps tie together the story you just told. For a Coming to America tale, a nice touch would be a picture of descendants from the ancestor, especially if you have a picture of multiple generations in a single shot. With this chapter's example, a long, drawn-out ending isn't needed, so it's easy to add a copy of the standard closing clip to end the film. Figure 6-6 shows the timeline after this step.

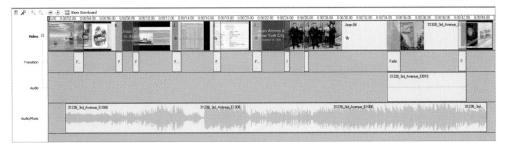

Figure 6-6 The timeline is complete with all the clips added to it.

Step 8: Finish It

Depending on how you intend to share your movie, you can select different options for your movie files. If you'll be sharing the files over the Internet, then selecting a low bit rate will be best to create a small movie file. If you'll be burning the movie to CD or DVD or viewing it on your own computer, then bit rate and file size is less important. In this chapter's example, the movie was initially created at 640 × 480 pixels, and the 45-second film created a file that was 5 megabytes (MB) in size. Even though the file is going to be shared over the Internet, the original documents are readable at the larger resolution.

So, it might be a trade-off: keep the larger file size so the images are clearly readable, but realize that the movie might be going over slow Internet connections to relatives in Europe. It might also be easier to burn the film to CD or DVD and mail the disc to the relatives. The best thing is that, using Movie Maker, you're not locked into one choice. You can create the movie in multiple formats and resolutions at any time.

If you're uploading a movie to a Web site, you can provide links to the original documents and your research sources, and you can add information about your movie or the research that complements the movie you just made. You can create a family tree on a Web page and then provide movie links for the people and projects directly on the tree. Genealogy is definitely an area where you can create movies and projects that bring together families and build a sense of pride in who you are and where you came from. Have fun!

- See Camcorders from a Different Angle

- Turbo-Charge Movie Maker and Your Movie
  Studio with Added Software

What the Manuals Didn't Tell You

CHAPTER 7

Once you become more comfortable with Movie Maker 2 and making movies, you'll never learn enough about certain topics. While the multimedia evolution continues, new hardware and software emerges each month that tugs at your mind, heart, and wallet. In this chapter, we'll explore a couple of those areas.

Around every corner is a better camcorder model or newer piece of software.

Coming Attractions

For many people, making movies is synonymous with using a camcorder. Your camcorder might be the primary reason you're now getting into digital video editing and Windows Movie Maker 2. Camcorders and computers have gotten so much more powerful and affordable in recent years, and computer-based movie editing has become so easy. If you've been putting off movie making for any reason, now is a perfect time to start. Using Movie Maker 2, you can take a digital camcorder, connect it to your computer's Apple FireWire port, and within minutes be capturing video from the camcorder and editing it in Movie Maker.

If you have an analog or digital camcorder, you've already experienced the joy of taking and watching your personal video footage. If your camcorder is analog, you might be thinking about moving to a digital one. The trend from analog to digital camcorders continues. The July 2003 issue of *Computer Videomaker* magazine contained the article "From Analog to Digital: A Six-Year Shift," which summarized the number of consumer models in the marketplace. In the span of six years, the market went from nearly all analog camcorders with only a few digital models to almost the opposite, with many more digital camcorder models today than analog.

You can also see this trend in online newsgroups. The single biggest topic on the *microsoft.public.windowsxp.moviemaker* newsgroup is camcorders, with about 13 percent of the postings discussing some aspect of them. The postings are about 115 models from eight brands, most of them Sony models.

NOTE

You can find out a lot of good information about camcorder technology online. Some of the best sites are run by pros and semi-pros. Check out *http://www.simplydv.co.uk*, *http://www.greatdv.com*, and *http://desktopvideo.about.com/cs/cameras* for more information.

Figure 7-1 shows a newer Sony TRV80 mini-DV camcorder that was used for several examples in this book. If you're thinking about buying a new digital camcorder or upgrading from analog to digital, you can find a lot of user information and people's experiences on the Microsoft newsgroup. You can also find extracts from the Microsoft newsgroups at *http://www.papajohn.org*, which is a good source for summaries and the most recent information so you don't need to search for it elsewhere.

Figure 7-1 The Sony TRV80 mini-DV camcorder has great features and is easy to use.

Learning About Camcorders and Capture Devices

Analog and digital camcorders look pretty much alike to the casual viewer. Data storage can be either analog or digital, and you can't always tell which format it is just by looking at the tape. Analog models often have the word "digital" someplace on the box or camcorder. What makes them different, and why are those differences important?

UNDERSTANDING MAGNETIC TAPES

With the advent of analog camcorders, magnetic tapes replaced the use of film for storing the data flowing into the camcorder lens. Digital camcorders started by continuing the tradition of using magnetic tapes. However, instead of recording and interpreting analog variations based on light and sound levels, digital camcorders laid the information down as data—streams of 1s and 0s that in turn make up the bits and bytes that describe a digital image and the associated audio.

Although magnetic tape can degrade and weaken with time and usage, digital images are less susceptible to data loss than analog tapes, which use analog signal strength to describe the encoded data.

Most of today's camcorders use one of three tape cartridges, which vary in size and shape:

- The larger 8 millimeter (mm) tapes, the top one in Figure 7-2, are about the size of an audio cassette tape. They're used in analog 8 mm, analog Hi8, and digital 8 camcorders. When used in an analog camcorder, these tapes can store two hours of video. When in a digital 8 camcorder, they go twice as fast and store one hour of video. The tape can be moved between analog and digital camcorders, recording some analog footage and some digital. The digital 8 information on these tapes is in the Digital Video–Audio Video Interleave (DV-AVI) format, which is the highest-quality consumer digital video format.

- The smaller 6.35 mm tapes, the bottom one in Figure 7-2, are used by mini-DV camcorders. The tapes also hold one hour of video of the same quality as the digital 8 tapes. Mini-DV camcorders are smaller than the digital 8 models. The mini-digital models are at the "sweet spot" of today's camcorder market, providing the highest consumer video resolution in a convenient camcorder size.

- The smallest tapes and camcorders are the micro-digital ones. They also store one hour of video, but because of their smaller size, they can't hold the highest image quality. To fit the information onto the smaller tape, the camcorder uses a compressed MPEG-2 format. These models are good for playback but not as good as the digital 8 and mini-DV models if you're planning to edit the footage into movies. The compressed format doesn't provide sufficient digital information to do high-quality digital editing.

Even when you use a digital camcorder to record clips or movies, don't assume that all digital camcorders are the same or that the quality of the video they record is the same. Movie quality can vary significantly among camcorder manufacturers, depending on the components used and the quality of the camcorder assembly.

The 8 mm models offered a good transition period between analog 8 mm and Hi8 models and the newer digital 8 ones. But today, they're being phased out of the marketplace in favor of the smaller mini-DV models.

Other recording methods are being developed. Some newer camcorders record directly onto CDs or DVDs. In these cases, the file is also compressed enough to fit a reasonable amount of footage on the disc. The quality of these videos is lower than DV-AVI, and (like micro-camcorders) the source material is less suitable for editing.

Figure 7-2 An 8 mm (digital 8) and a 6.35 mm (mini-DV) camcorder tape

UNDERSTANDING CAMCORDER OPTICAL SYSTEMS

All camcorders need to gather light through optical lenses and focus the image onto a recording mechanism inside. The quality of the optical system, differences in optical zooming, automatic light and focus adjustments, and other camcorder features make for differences among various models. Those differences can affect the image sharpness, color rendition, and low-light capabilities.

Higher-end analog camcorders might have solid benefits when compared to some of today's lower-end digital ones. They might be better suited for low-light situations or when a high degree of zoom is needed. There are many lenses and peripherals available for analog cameras, and they might have solid overall construction quality.

Today's digital camcorders are producing professional-quality images that weren't possible only a few years ago in consumer models. Advances in electronics and manufacturing are producing smaller camcorders that are point-and-shoot friendly, with plenty of menus and help screens to walk users through the camera settings. Digital camcorders tend to be lighter weight, which can be a relief when shooting extended scenes without a tripod or just carrying around the camcorder on a vacation.

UNDERSTANDING CAMCORDER AUDIO SYSTEMS

As you'd expect, many consumer-grade analog camcorders record only in monaural sound, not stereo, though some higher-end analog ones have built-in stereo microphones or could use an external stereo mike for stereo sound. About half of today's digital camcorders record stereo sound using a built-in microphone, but audio quality can vary—although stereo is a "nice to have" feature, there aren't too many hobby or casual filming events that require stereo instead of mono. It's also difficult for manufacturers to make a small camcorder and also have high-quality audio recording capability built into the camcorder case; admittedly, most of the money is spent on the optical and electronic components. But most digital camcorders will record perfectly serviceable audio for nearly all occasions.

UNDERSTANDING VIDEO CAPTURE CARDS

To retrieve your video clips from a digital camcorder, your computer will need a video capture card that accepts a digital stream from your camcorder. The most popular type of capture cards use IEEE 1394 connections. FireWire is the most common market name for this type of connection, while Sony i.LINK is another; these names are synonymous with each other and work the same. IEEE 1394 is the best connection and cable type for video capture cards and for camcorders because it can handle streaming data reliably.

IEEE 1394 connections on laptops usually have smaller four-pin connections, the same as those at the other end of the cable that attaches to the camcorder. Desktop computers usually have similar but wider connections and use six pins. When connecting a camcorder to a computer via FireWire, you might need a four-pin to six-pin cable or a four-pin to four-pin cable. Or, if you use both a desktop and laptop for movie work, you might need one of each.

Figure 7-3 shows a laptop's FireWire connection at the left, next to the Universal Serial Bus (USB) connection being used for the mouse.

Figure 7-3 Four-pin FireWire connection on a laptop computer

Less common are USB connections that connect digital camcorders directly to computers without requiring a video capture card; however, special software is still needed to handle the data stream. In recent months, more camcorders are supporting USB connections because people frequently have USB hubs for other peripherals such as digital cameras or MP3 players. USB 2.0 is the only type capable of supporting high-quality digital video; USB 1.1 or earlier is too slow and unreliable to support streaming data from a camcorder to a computer.

If you don't have an appropriate video capture card, you'll have to purchase and install it before being able to transfer video files. See the installation instructions for your capture card for more information.

> **Don't** attempt to install a video capture card unless you first turn off and unplug your computer! You can easily damage the computer or give yourself a potentially lethal shock from the electrical voltage inside a computer case. Read the instructions for your capture card and computer before attempting to install the card and follow all warnings, precautions, and instructions. If you have any doubts about this task, ask a computer professional to help you.
>
> **WARNING**

Movie Maker 2 doesn't capture video from micro-camcorders or those that record directly to CD or DVD because they use the MPEG-2 or other proprietary file formats. You have to use the software that comes with those camcorders and do conversions to align the video files with formats that Movie Maker can import. See Chapter 4 for additional information about format conversions.

UNDERSTANDING ANALOG VIDEO CAPTURE

Capturing analog video from analog camcorders, VCRs, and TVs requires specialized hardware or software that usually doesn't come with a computer. The best way is to purchase a special analog-to-digital capture card that you can use directly with your analog camcorder; this will produce the best results for your capturing sessions. The *http://www.papajohn.org* Web site has a section about analog video capture, with information about a dozen companies that provide such conversion devices.

UNDERSTANDING CONVERTING ANALOG TAPES TO DIGITAL

Most digital 8 camcorders can play back 8 mm and Hi8 analog tapes, doing the necessary conversion of the analog signal to a digital one. If you have older 8 mm or Hi8 analog tapes and want to import them into Movie Maker 2, you can capture the analog video directly to the computer using the same digital capture process; no additional hardware or software is needed. This compatibility is only found with 8 mm, Hi8, and digital 8 camcorder models. The quality of the Hi8 video is a bit lower than digital 8 but still higher than normal TV playback. Even on computer playback, it's often difficult to tell the difference in quality between Hi8 and digital 8 video clips.

> **NOTE**
>
> If you use a digital camcorder and a video capture card to play back and record an analog tape, a few of the bottom horizontal lines might not be in sync with the rest of the video image. This is an artifact of the conversions that are required to process the data stream. Consider such lines as normal.

Saving or exporting the movie to your digital 8 or mini-digital camcorder tape is an ideal way to store your finished movies or edited source files. It's the most practical way to retain a copy in the highest-quality format. Reasons for tape storage include the following:

- Having the highest quality original video available for use in future editing sessions or for burning more CDs or DVDs from the highest-quality source

- Using the digital camcorder to plug into a TV or VCR for playing back or copying to VCR tapes

- Archival or backup purposes

CD storage is convenient for really short DV-AVI clips, not for short or long movies. DVDs use highly compressed files that are great for distribution, but not sufficient for high-quality archiving. If you're serious about keeping your source files or finished movies around in the highest-possible quality, then you should save the files back to your camcorder.

Chapter 5 covers the steps for saving a movie onto a digital camcorder tape using Movie Maker.

Turbo-Charging Movie Maker

You can make amazing movies using Movie Maker 2 with the basic software features that are included in it. But, if you already know you want additional items that extend the basic features, you can download and install them from the respective supplier's Web sites. The following sections highlight five software packages currently available from Microsoft and others that you can use to enhance your movie making.

INSTALLING WINDOWS MOVIE MAKER 2 CREATIVITY FUN PACK

The Movie Maker 2 Creativity Fun Pack is a free download from Microsoft and contains many creative extras, including video titles, music, and sound effects. Whatever the occasion, there's something that'll help you make your home movies even better:

Titles and end credits   Choose from a selection of six countdown, ending, and blank video titles to add to your home movies. Use the blank clips as backgrounds when you add your own text overlays in Movie Maker.

Static video titles   The package contains 16 static title slides you can use as is or add your own titles to. These slides cover many occasions, including Mother's Day, Father's Day, and graduation.

Music tracks and music transitions   The package has three full-length songs you can add to any kind of movie. There are also five music transitions to add dramatic interest to your home movies.

Sound effects   Choose from more than 50 new sound effects, including party sounds, graduation ceremony sounds, and a bunch of miscellaneous sounds, such as cars, buzzers, and clicks.

You can download the Movie Maker 2 Creativity Fun Pack by clicking Help | Movie Maker On The Web. Follow the links to download the package. When you install it, there will be a new folder on your hard disk with lots of sample clips in various subfolders:

- Music Tracks and Music Transitions
- Sound Effects
- Static Titles
- Video Titles and End Credits

Click Start | All Programs | Windows XP Creativity Fun Packs | Windows Movie Maker 2. The four folders will be listed, and you can click any folder to view the contents. You can then import these clips into Movie Maker 2 as you do other source files. Figure 7-4 shows the blue five-second countdown clip being used in Movie Maker.

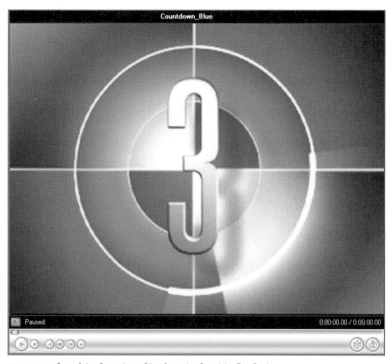

Figure 7-4 One of the Countdown Clips from the Creativity Fun Pack

INSTALLING MICROSOFT PLUS! DIGITAL MEDIA EDITION

Microsoft Plus! packs have long been known for their fun additions to Microsoft operating systems. The packs contain additional consumer-oriented features and program add-ons for putting more color, zip, and fun into using Windows. The Plus! Digital Media Edition includes the Plus! Effects & Transitions for Windows Movie Maker 2, which contains 25 new video effects and 25 new video transitions. You can use Plus! video effects to add exotic colors, vivid streaks and spots, wild textures, and more to your Windows Movie Maker 2 videos and pictures. Plus! video transitions make your movies even more fun. Use them to add unique and captivating transitions between video clips.

You can purchase the Microsoft Plus! Digital Media Edition via a download from the Microsoft Web site. Click Help, Movie Maker On The Web. Follow the links to purchase and download the Plus! Pack. Make sure Movie Maker 2 is closed before you install the Plus! Digital Media Edition. When you're finished, the additional items are automatically added to your collections.

Figure 7-5 shows the list of video effects added by the Plus! software, with the Plus! Texture effect being previewed in the monitor.

Figure 7-5 The Plus! Digital Media Edition adds exciting new transitions and effects to your collections.

INSTALLING PIXÉLAN SPICEFX PACKS

You can expect to see many third-party effects developed as the popularity of Movie Maker 2 increases. Pixélan Software at *http://www.pixelan.com* has already produced a number of SpiceFX Packs for Movie Maker 2. The Pan/Zoom Effects package is of particular interest to movie makers looking for more powerful effects and transitions. It's a set of more than 60 effects that you can use to pan and zoom into or out of specific points of interest on a video clip or still image. The Pan/Zoom Effects package, and the other Movie Maker add-ons, are available for trial use or purchase, are easy to download and install, and are installed automatically like the Plus! package. Download one of the trial packages to see if you like the additional effects and transitions. The trial versions are fully functional, but a big "X" appears on the finished clip until you purchase the retail version.

Figure 7-6 shows one of the video effects from the Pan/Zoom Effects pack, the latest to be released by Pixélan. The larger picture in the monitor shows how the picture appears at the beginning of the clip when the Pan/Zoom CenterR > CenterL effect is selected. The smaller insert shows the ending position after the image is panned from right to left.

Figure 7-6 The Pixélan Pan/Zoom package adds the ability to create dynamic camera movements in your clips.

INSTALLING VIRTUALDUB

VirtualDub, a free download from *http://www.virtualdub.org*, is one of the utilities you can use to "preprocess" your clips before importing them into Movie Maker. VirtualDub's effects let you heavily modify a clip, including cropping, resizing, blurring, changing clip color, and adjusting brightness or contrast. You can also do some of its many capabilities within Movie Maker; but one of the benefits of using a utility such as VirtualDub is that you can apply effects to clips before you render the final movie. This helps speed up the rendering process, which can be important if you have a large movie and a slower computer.

Figure 7-7 shows VirtualDub in action. In this case, a 640 × 480–sized video clip is being resized to an unusual 640 × 200 pixel dimension, and at the same time being rotated by 10 degrees, with any resulting space around the new video being filled with a selected blue color. The figure shows the before and after video clip in a preview mode within VirtualDub.

INSTALLING IRFANVIEW

Everyone who does multimedia work has his or her personal "Swiss Army knife" for pictures or videos. Although Movie Maker 2 is great for working with video, other programs are better suited for working with individual images or still pictures. IrfanView

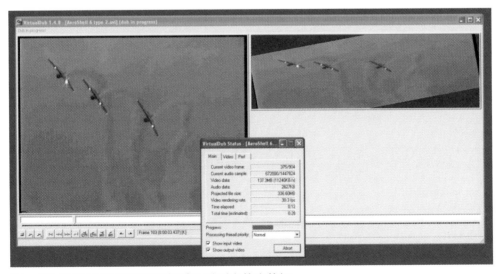

Figure 7-7 Working a clip with VirtualDub before using it in Movie Maker

is a compact, easy-to-use image viewer and editor with many built-in filters and effects. It's a free download from *http://www.irfanview.com*. IrfanView can open many file types that can't be directly imported into Movie Maker 2 and then save the images as a compatible file type. It can even open Adobe Photoshop and Jasc Software's Paint Shop Pro files so you can make a copy for Movie Maker or crop a portion of an existing image file. Figure 7-8 shows an 800 × 600 pixel area being cropped out of a much larger picture.

One of IrfanView's incredibly handy features is the ability to do batch conversions. Batch conversions apply the same changes to a group of files at once, so you don't have to open each one individually, make the changes, and then save the file. Batch conversion can include resizing and resampling images so the size and resolution match the one you're using for your movies. This is extremely handy if you're making a low-bandwidth version for distribution over the Internet and prefer to use 320 × 240 pixel images as source files. There are also a number of special effects included in IrfanView so you can manipulate and change your image quickly and easily before you import it into Movie Maker.

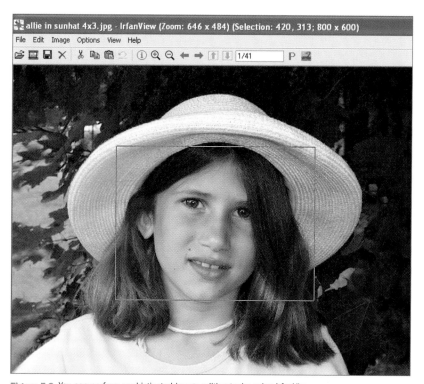

Figure 7-8 You can perform sophisticated image editing tasks using IrfanView.

GOING PRO

One of the great advantages of Movie Maker 2 is that it gives you a solid, powerful set of tools to produce professional-looking videos for your family and friends. Using add-ins and third-party programs can enhance your ability to produce high-quality videos that look like a million bucks.

In addition to the software covered in this chapter, there are professional video editing packages available that are priced at a professional level. If you become serious about video, you may want to consider moving up to one of these programs. Here is what the extra money buys you:

- More video tracks and sophisticated editing tools
- Ability to design and create custom transitions and effects

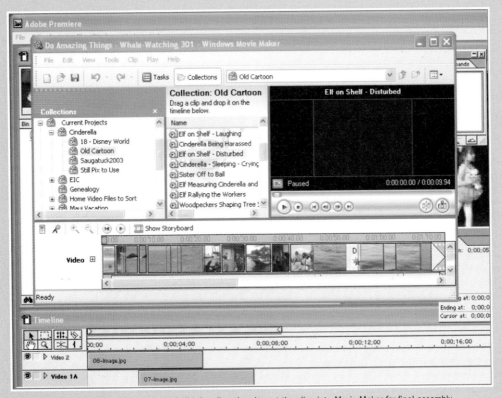

You can use a combination of programs to build the clips, then import the clips into Movie Maker for final assembly.

- Add animations and special text effects to film clips

- Sophisticated audio tools including panning, mixing, and multi-channel editing capabilities

- Special effects such as matte, chromakey, and masks

- Support for professional cameras, recording, and playback equipment

Of course, you don't need to step up to this level of editing in order to make great movies. In fact, it's more cost-effective if you can use a professional suite to work on clips, then import them into Movie Maker for final assembly. This is often the case if you are taking a class in movie making, or if a friend has a copy of a professional editing program that you can borrow, such as the one in the graphic on the previous page.

Most of the time it's far easier to use Movie Maker to do the assembly and rendering of a movie than to figure out the nuances and option settings for a professional-quality program. If you want to use a professional program for a clip or two, most pro suites can save to AVI or MPEG format, which can then be imported into Movie Maker.

Should you like IrfanView and its ability to work with still images, you can download additional plug-ins from the Internet.

One added feature, available as a plug-in, is a multimedia player that has a great frame extraction feature. Open a video clip in IrfanView's multimedia player, and select the frame extraction option. It'll tell you how many frames there are, let you pick the starting and ending frame numbers, and then make a full-sized TIF picture of each frame in your selected group. You can then edit, crop, or manipulate the image further before you save it and import it into Movie Maker. This feature gives you a lot of control over still images, more so than the Take Picture feature in Movie Maker itself.

IrfanView's multimedia player can only do frame extractions from DV-AVI type II files. Movie Maker 2 creates type I files, so you need to convert the movie into a type II file first. See *http://www.papajohn.org* for current pointers to tools that can do such conversions, one of which is Movie Maker 1.

ADDING OTHER SOFTWARE

As Movie Maker 2 gains in popularity, many software packages will become available to work directly or indirectly with Movie Maker. The following are a few other downloads that enhance both movie making and movie viewing on your personal computer:

Windows Media Player 9   The new version is a fast and flexible player of audio and video files that's optimized for Windows XP. It's an upgrade of the player that came with Windows XP and a free download from Microsoft. You can use Windows Update to automatically upgrade the player; click Start | All Programs | Windows Update. Have it scan your computer, and then select Windows Media Player 9 when presented with your download options. Alternatively, you can go to *http://www.microsoft.com/windowsxp/windowsmediaplayer*, and then go to the Downloads section to get the full player.

Codecs   Movie Maker 2 and Windows Media Player automatically obtain any additionally needed Microsoft codecs if you're connected directly to the Internet. Earlier versions of Windows Media Player, such as those on Windows 9x or

Windows NT, do not support playback of movies made using the version 9 codecs. If you have an older player, you might want to download the full version 9 codec set. These codecs were developed and issued by Microsoft in parallel with the rollout of Movie Maker 2. The package is available for download at *http:// www.microsoft.com/windows/windowsmedia/format/codecdownload.aspx.*

HighMAT viewer If you use Movie Maker to burn a CD, you'll add the movie to the CD and create a menu structure that's aligned with the new HighMAT technology. You can install this stand-alone viewer, available from the HighMAT organization, and use it to effectively view the CD on your computer or others that run the Windows XP operating system. It's a free download from *http://www.highmat.com.* The simulation is all that's available today because the current DVD players with the HighMAT logo don't yet include WMV file support. The viewer plays only on Windows XP.

Glossary

mini-DV	Short for "mini–digital video." This format uses 6.35 mm tape, so the cameras can be made smaller and lighter than 8 mm camcorders.
pan	Short for "panorama." This was originally used to mean keeping the camera stationary and pivoting it from one side to the other and capturing a panorama scene. Today it means to move the camera to follow an object or to create a panorama effect.
USB	The acronym for "Universal Serial Bus." This is a specification for connecting computer peripherals and other electronic devices together. It's similar to FireWire, using slower data transfer speeds, but is more popular and found on many other devices besides digital video.
zoom	To change the focus relative to an object so that the apparent distance is closer (zoom in) or farther (zoom out) from the object.

- **Come Up with Your Big Idea**
- **Nail the Script**
- **See Your Story Emerge Using Your Storyboard**
- **Set Up Your Preproduction**
- **Set Up Your Production**
- **Set Up Your Postproduction**

Running the Show from the Director's Chair

CHAPTER 8

When you strip away all the glamour, bright lights, and celebrities, movies are all about storytelling. People want to hear stories. Like kids who won't go to sleep until you read to them, people from all walks of life will stop what they're doing if there's the promise of a good story. Movies make a bargain with viewers: if you give me a few moments of your time, I'll entertain you with a story so you can put aside your cares for a little while.

You don't have to limit yourself to the "real world" when storytelling.

Coming Attractions

What a great bargain! As the person with the camera, you're in the perfect position to be a storyteller. If you think you'd like to do more than just shoot pictures, then you might be ready to move on to the "top dog" challenge—becoming the director of your own movie.

Most of this book has focused on making a story out of existing film footage, in effect retrofitting your story idea onto events and activities that have already happened. This chapter works in the other direction: start with the story, and then figure out how to capture the footage necessary to tell your story on the big or little screen.

What's the Big Idea?

Every movie starts with an idea. It could be a funny joke you heard, something that happened to a relative, an incident at work, or maybe some gossip between friends. All of a sudden something goes "click!" in your head, and you have the flash of an idea. It usually starts like, "Wouldn't it be cool if I made a movie about...." In fact, great films have been started from less.

Ideas are wonderful because they're an inexhaustible supply of material for movies. You can turn nearly any idea into a movie because it's not the idea that's unique but how you tell the story around that idea. "Boy meets girl" is quite possibly the world's oldest story idea, but it has spawned such different stories as Shakespeare's *Romeo and Juliet* and Nora Ephron's *When Harry Met Sally*.

Your idea can be about a person, whether fictional or someone you admire; about places or events that have impacted your life; or about a story you've been itching to put to film. All of these are great areas to explore, and with the luxury of your own camera and your own editing studio, you can move the ideas out of your head and into the real world.

> If your big idea is about someone in the real world and not a fictional character, you'll need to secure the rights to the story or obtain a release from that person to make a story about them. Check with an entertainment law attorney for advice on how to proceed with these kinds of ideas.

TIP

You don't have to limit yourself to the "real world" when storytelling. The "Mr. Bill" series of comedy sketches on NBC's *Saturday Night Live* used nothing more than Play-Doh, a pair of hands, and props such as rolling pins to wreak havoc on the clay world of Mr. Bill. Look around your home to see if you could have fun with other toys and games. Use LEGOs to tell your story, use plastic army men, or even use construction paper puppets (see Figure 8-1). Anything is fair game for you and your creativity!

Figure 8-1 You can use toys to tell your story, if you can arrange for a loan from a local kid.

It's All in the Script

Once you have an idea, it's time to write it down to see what it'll look like. The script is the basis for all the other aspects of directing a film. It's a roadmap that describes the details of your story, including descriptions of the scenes, dialogue between characters, and notes or directions to you for production and postproduction about special effects or sound effects.

It seems like a lot, but don't worry; writing a script isn't as scary as it sounds! You don't need fancy scriptwriting software or need to take classes in how to be a professional screenplay writer. Instead, spend your time writing down what you (and your actors or others helping you on your movie) need to know to get your movie onto your camcorder.

TIP

If you really want to create a professional-looking script, you can learn about formatting scripts, writing scripts, and even using scriptwriting software or add-ins for Microsoft Word in many books and online resources. You can also purchase scripts of movies to study the format and content. Search online bookstores or the Web for these script resources.

Because you're telling a story, you should have a beginning, a middle, and an end. The beginning sets the scene, background, or environment, and it describes or sets off the crisis or initial conflict. The middle has obstacles or challenges to resolving the conflict. The end resolves the conflict (either for better or worse).

You can cast nearly anything in the beginning-middle-end format. For example:

Beginning   Two campers are walking through the woods when a huge brown bear suddenly appears in the clearing about 50 feet in front of them. (This sets the scene and introduces the conflict.)

Middle   The bear sees the campers and begins to head toward them. The first guy drops his backpack, digs out a pair of sneakers, and frantically begins to put them on. The second guy says, "What are you doing? Sneakers won't help you outrun that bear." (This increases the threat, adding challenges to escape.)

End   "I don't need to outrun the bear," the first guy says. "I just need to outrun you." (The conflict is resolved—or at least it is for one of the two guys.)

Just reading the previous sequence can give you ideas of what your script should contain. It should have information about the actors (two guys and a bear or bear substitute), the location (woods), and the props (backpack and sneakers).

One way to help you write your script is to remember that the entire movie already exists; you just need to describe what you see as you play back the movie in your head. You don't need to go overboard on details or precision because much of this information will be worked out by you and others helping you with your movie.

Storyboards: Seeing Your Story Emerge

A storyboard is a series of drawings that take a camera-eye view of your script, showing you what the camera "sees." The storyboard illustrations can be anything from stick figures and rough drawings to finely detailed artwork. Most people like to try sketching key shots from each scene in the script to help give an idea of where the actors should be positioned or what the camera angle will be. Storyboards aren't mandatory but are a valuable tool for anyone making a movie.

You can use just about anything to create storyboards, including drawing tools in Microsoft Word, Microsoft PowerPoint, or even Microsoft Paint. For more formal-looking storyboards, there's software available that lets you use predrawn figures and objects. Search the Web for storyboard software for more information.

Depending on the detail, storyboards also give ideas for scouting locations or interiors for any sets you might need. You can show details about costumes and environments so that your actors and assistants can get a feeling for the kind of "look" you want in your movie.

If you don't have any drawing skills, that's okay; you're not creating a work of art or seeking approval from your art teacher. And your movie might be short enough that you don't need to sketch any details for the shoot. But it's a worthwhile exercise to work through at least once so you can get a feeling for how things should look and get the images out of your head and onto paper.

Preproduction: Cheap Is Good!

Now that your idea is written down, you've drafted some kind of script, and maybe you even have a few storyboards put together, it's time to decide whether it's a "go" or a "no go" on your movie. If you want to go for it, then great—it's time to start putting all the pieces together for your magnum opus!

Preproduction is the phase where you start figuring out what you need for your movie, what it'll cost, where the work will take place, and who will help you.

MAKING A BUDGET

You need to evaluate your budget (it's rare that movies can be made for free) and see if you can spend the money or time needed to make your story a reality. If you've never made a movie before, it's hard to know what materials and equipment will cost down the road or how much you should allocate to them. Some of this you'll learn with experience while you shoot scenes and figure out the rough cost per scene or per day. Other aspects you'll learn the hard way after a vital piece of equipment breaks and must be replaced.

One of the best tips for creating a budget is to assume you have no money. This might not be precisely true, but it forces you to be creative with your movie. Instead of planning an Elizabethan costume drama that takes place on location at various castles and churches in England, you should plan on a more scaled-down approach, begging or borrowing as much as you can to support your film. Hang an Oriental rug up in the garage, move a few pieces of older furniture in, and you've got an Elizabethan drawing room with a wall tapestry. Ask to borrow period clothes from your local community college or theater group. Or better yet, reframe your story to a less expensive time period. The movie *West Side Story* was a musical retelling of *Romeo and Juliet*; if you reframe your story, can you still tell an effective story without the expense?

TIP

A rule of thumb you can use to figure a budget for any movie project is to make rough guesstimates of what everything will cost. Now double that figure. Now add 20 percent. You now stand a chance of being somewhere in the ballpark for the final cost of making your movie.

Look for many ways to avoid incurring costs for your movie. The "Mr. Bill" comedy sketches had very low costs; the "Bear Joke" outlined earlier could also be filmed for very low cost. Don't forget about the popular movie, *The Blair Witch Project*, which was shot in the woods using a few handheld cameras, three actors, and props everyone already owned; everyone camped in the woods for eight straight days of filming—no four-star hotels for the cast on that shoot!

Even if you have the money, resist the temptation to throw dollars at everything. You'll have a much more satisfactory film-making experience and be prouder of the finished result when you can say, "See that rock? It's a big chunk of Styrofoam we painted gray and rolled in the dirt while it was still wet."

SCOUTING LOCATIONS AND SETS

A location is any place in your film where you tell the story, whether interior or exterior. In the movie industry, a location is anything not on a movie soundstage. A soundstage is used instead to build sets that represent a particular location—a bustling newsroom, the heroine's apartment, the mad scientist's laboratory. Movie makers prefer using soundstages for much of the work because they can control every aspect of the set's appearance and sound quality, and they have access to tools, shops, and crew who can rig and light the sets. As a beginning filmmaker, you probably don't have the money to rent time at a soundstage and build the necessary sets, so your soundstage may be your own unfinished basement or garage. Again, if you're thinking low cost, you should make every effort to find locations that fit your needs, rather than assume you can throw money at the problem and solve it. Maybe you're on vacation and can use pictures from an exotic locale. Or, maybe you can "edit" a couple of photos to add to your location's visual interst (see Figure 8-2).

Locations can be very costly in terms of money and time. In an ideal world, you find the perfect location for every scene in your film; in the real world, locations are rarely perfect, and there always seems to be some reason you can't use them. The perfect witchy-looking house for your Halloween film is unavailable because the owner is as nasty as the exterior is spooky. That street scene you want to shoot in a perfect turn-of-the-century neighborhood is next to a freeway overpass, making your audio unusable. You can't shoot in the local park without obtaining a permit from the city. Problems such as these are very common, forcing you to rethink parts of your script to see if the locations can be changed or, in the extreme scenario, if the scene can be removed from the script entirely.

Figure 8-2 Sometimes you don't have to go very far to find a great location.

The time factor enters into play when you consider traveling, setting up, and tearing down for each of your locations. If you have eight locations in your movie and you want to shoot them all in a weekend, you have to shoot all the scenes for four locations on Saturday with the same schedule on Sunday. Even if you live in a small town, figure on at least an hour to pack things up, move everyone to the new location, and set up again for the next scene. That's four hours out of your schedule so far, and you have yet to shoot a single foot of tape. Add a lot more time per location if you live in a major metropolitan area.

If logistics such as these start impacting your budget or shooting schedule, it's time to revisit your script and be ruthless about the number of locations you have. Is your script truly at the bare minimum needed to tell the story? Can you compress two locations into one? Do outdoor scenes have to be outdoors, or can they move to an interior location and not damage the storyline?

Other aspects to consider for your locations are access to electrical power for lights and camera equipment, ease of access for cast and crew, and any permits or regulations that might govern how and when you use the area.

ROUNDING UP YOUR CAST AND CREW

Cast and crew are the people who help make your vision a reality. The cast is made up of your actors, with speaking or nonspeaking roles, and the crew are the people who help you with the technical details of filming.

If you've written down your script, you'll give copies to your actors and crew so they can do their respective jobs. Actors need to learn their lines, and the crew needs to figure out how many locations are needed and how to light them, record the sound, and set props. You can hold auditions for your actors, or you can cast your friends and family as the players in your movie. The crew can be people who work in the filmmaking industry, or they can be friends from across the street.

If you're still thinking cheaply, you ideally use actors who can also set up lights, carry equipment, consult on camera angles, or even apply makeup if needed.

The following are a couple key points to remember about your cast and crew:

Have decent food and beverages available   Unless you're paying your cast and crew wages for their work, they're probably working for you for free and thus donating their time for your movie. A great way to show your appreciation is to have decent food and beverages for them between takes or at mealtimes. Not only will they thank you for having their welfare in mind (especially if you have hot food and beverages during an outdoor shoot), this will also cut down on the "I'm just running to the store for a sandwich" errands that inevitably creep in and delay your shooting schedule (see Figure 8-3).

Figure 8-3 Food is always welcome on a movie set.

Say "please" and "thank you"   As tempting as it might be to adopt the infamous Hollywood-size ego and start bellowing at your minions, don't. These people are doing you a favor by helping you on your movie; if you get nasty, they can pack up and leave at any time, leaving you in the lurch without cast or crew and holding a bunch of footage that you can't use anymore. Common politeness, along with liberal usage of "please" and "thank you," will go a long way to making the process enjoyable. One of the best compliments you can hear is, "When are you making your next movie? I'd like to help out on that one, too."

Production: Fun on the Run

This is it. This is what all your planning has been about. You've got your script, you've found your locations and actors, you've even figured out how far away the nearest pizza delivery place is. Now you're ready to go out and film your movie!

LIGHTS, CAMERA, ACTION!

When you're filming your movie, you can take several actions to make your life a lot easier. These are lessons learned over the years by professional moviemakers, and you can take advantage of their experience to help your movie flow smoothly and professionally:

Film all the scenes at each location at one time   Many people think movies and television shows are shot in the order they're viewed on the screen. If you think about it a moment, it would be very inefficient; the crew would set up at one location, shoot the scene, tear down and move to another location, shoot the scene, tear down and move back to the first location, shoot it, tear down and move back to the second location…. So much time would be spent setting up and tearing down that nothing would be produced. A shooting schedule is created in preproduction that collects all the scenes at a particular location and organizes them so that setup and teardown are minimized. This way, all the scenes in a drawing room, for example, are shot using the same setup, even though they take place at different times in the story.

Use coverage to get all the angles and shots you need from a single scene   The concept of "coverage" refers to filming from multiple angles to maximize the amount of footage from a scene for later use in editing. For example, if you have two people in a scene, you'd run through the scene once, with the camera focusing on both actors. Then you'd run the scene a second time, focusing on the first actor. Then you'd run the scene a third time, focusing on the second actor. Figure 8-4 shows everyone just getting into position. If you had multiple cameras available, you'd run all the cameras at once for the scene rather than doing multiple takes. Of course, there may be problems with the scene, so you'll probably need to run multiple takes anyway.

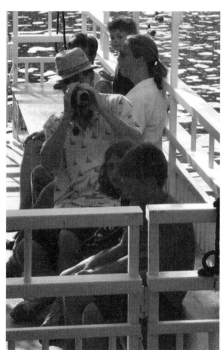

You now have the ability during editing to show both actors or to switch between actors to see their reactions to each other. If you have more actors in the scene, you increase the number of angles and number of times you need to run through the scene in order to get enough coverage. You might be able to get away with not filming actors in the background or those who don't actively participate in the scene.

You can see that a day's shoot can quickly be eaten up by coverage because you have to move the camera and lights each time you want to shoot a new angle on an actor.

Figure 8-4 Set up your actors and camera angles before you shoot each scene.

When you shoot coverage, you increase the shooting ratio of tape stock you need for your movie. If you have two actors, you have a 3:1 ratio, where you shoot three minutes of footage for each minute of finished movie. With five actors, you have a 5:1 ratio. Plan your coverage ahead of time, and make sure you have enough tape for the day's shoot, plus some extra just in case.

Shoot exteriors first If at all possible, shoot your exterior locations first and save the interiors for later in the schedule. The reason for this can be summed up in one word: weather. Among all the variables you can't control, the biggest one that can negatively affect your schedule is the weather. If you're shooting in the woods on Saturday and a big storm blows through, the wind and rain will make shooting impossible (see Figure 8-5). You'll need to reschedule for another day. If you leave your exteriors for last, then the bad weather may drag on, and on, and on...leaving you with a schedule that spins rapidly out of control. When you shoot your exteriors first, even if bad weather occurs, you have more chances to make up for it later in the schedule.

Figure 8-5 Bad weather can make for a messy shoot.

Interestingly, bright sunlight is one of the worst days you can try to shoot, especially if it's around noon. The best exterior days are ones with some overcast to help diffuse the light and soften any harsh shadows or outlines that can appear in the scene.

Keep a tape log A tape log is used to record the movie name, tape number, the time code, and the scene and take number. This is invaluable later when you're in editing mode and can't remember which tape had that one perfect take you need for your scene.

TIPS ON CAMERA HANDLING

The first rule is to use a tripod. Unless you're deliberately going for the handheld look, complete with bobbing and weaving around, you should use a tripod on every shot you shoot. If you don't have one available, do anything you can to brace the camcorder with something other than your back and arms. Use a fence, a rock, or a tree. Even with bracing the camera on your shoulder and leaning against a tree, the camera still moves with your breathing and with subtle muscle adjustments.

Another way to steady the scene in the viewfinder is to use a wider-angle shot. You can use this technique if you're taking video while sitting in a moving car. Zooming in and taking close-ups always magnifies the movements as it does the image, so zooming out reduces movement because it views a wider scene.

Don't use pan and zoom motions for your scenes. If you do pan, do it slowly, especially if you're shooting characters at a distance against a background. If you're following a soccer ball in the foreground or someone playing in the game, you can follow the person or object, but the background will blur.

If you zoom into a character or object, do it slowly so your audience won't get vertigo. A hard zoom is tougher to stop in focus, so if you misjudge the zoom, you'll need to redo the shot. If your camera uses optical zoom, stop before you get to the end of the optical zoom range. Digital zoom is nowhere near as good looking on video as optical zoom. You can use Movie Maker in postproduction to zoom in tighter than the optical zoom range.

For best results, don't use the autofocus option on your camera; do everything manually.

Make light of a situation   Lighting is critical in nearly any movie project, and the secret to great film making is the perfect marriage of smart camera work and smart lighting. Nearly all scenes, interior or exterior, will benefit from having two light sources focused on or around your actors. One is the key light, and the other is the fill light. The key light makes your actors visible and reveals details, and the fill light softens shadows and makes people look more natural. You don't need expensive professional lights to light the scene; using a little creativity, you can use trouble lights, flood lights, light-colored umbrellas, and those reflective items you put in car windows on hot days to be light sources for your scene.

Help your cast and crew make your movie   As the director, you must give the cast and crew enough information to bring the story to life. Have a few run-throughs of your script before you go out on a shoot, and then do a dry run for each scene so you can work out any issues with blocking, props, camera angles, lighting, and audio.

WHAT'S THAT NOISE?

Every filmmaker who has ever put frames to film has worried about the accompanying audio. Nothing can ruin your storytelling experience as much as taking all your tape into the editing studio, importing your footage, and then finding out the audio is nearly unusable. Traffic, wind, transient bird noises, overhead aircraft, or a bad microphone can put you in a bind. Do you reassemble everyone and go back to reshoot the scene? Do you bring the actors into your studio and rerecord the audio, hoping to overdub the scene? Or do you make do with what you have, grabbing the least offensive audio track from the scene coverage and hope that people don't cringe too much when they hear it?

None of these options are good ones, so the best way to avoid dilemmas in postproduction is to pay attention to your audio before and during the shoot. Most consumer-grade digital cameras

Figure 8-6 A good microphone will dramatically improve your audio quality.

have inexpensive microphones attached to capture the audio. You'll quickly find that these microphones excel at capturing almost anything but the actual dialogue or audio track you're trying to record. Fortunately, many cameras have audio or line-in connections you can use for an external microphone. Go buy a decent microphone, such as a directional mike with windscreens and extension cable (see Figure 8-6). Use this to record your audio. It'll remarkably improve your audio quality and give you better control.

> Many camcorders offer a menu setting choice of 12-bit or 16-bit audio recording modes. The 12-bit setting creates two sets of stereo tracks, and the 16-bit setting uses a single set of stereo tracks to produce CD-quality sound. If your camcorder footage is headed toward editing on a computer, use the 16-bit option.

TIP

COSTUMES, MAKEUP, AND PROPS

This is where your ability to scrounge comes in handy. You might need all three of these depending on your movie, and it's safe to say they don't come cheap. If your script deals with contemporary problems of a middle-class American family in 2004, then you don't need to roam far to find the outfits, furniture, homes, and trappings of everyday living. On the other hand, if you're attempting to re-create the adventures of futuristic space explorers in the Andromeda galaxy, you have a lot more work ahead of you because you'll have to create every item that comes into view on the screen.

You can be creative by asking your actors to do the work of providing their own costumes and props for the movie. With a script and some storyboards, you can list what's needed for each scene and then build a master list of costumes and props for your movie. You can circulate this list among family, friends, cast, and crew with a plea to find needed items. As with everything else, the more common it is, the easier it'll be to find or borrow the item. The less common, then the more creative you have to be to find it, build it, or come up with a substitute in the script for it. (Do you really need that Porsche 996 for the scene, or will another, cheaper sports car, as in Figure 8-7, do?)

Figure 8-7 Figure out creative substitutions for your movie.

IS THIS THING ON?

There you are, juggling your camcorder and microphone, trying to frame the shot and simultaneously set audio levels while your actors do a dry run-through of the scene. Once you're actually filming, are you paying attention to the image in the viewfinder or the sound in the background? If you're like most people, the image is of primary importance and the audio a distant second. Because audio is so important to the finished product, recording and monitoring audio is really a full-time job for a second person.

Your audio person should be equipped with a pair of headphones plugged into your camera's line-out jack or headphone jack, as shown below.

Most camcorders have jacks for external microphones and headsets. Use them.

Purchase an extensible painter's handle for use as a microphone boom, and either tape the mike or attach a proper fastener to the end for the mike. Your audio person is responsible for handling the boom mike during the scene and is responsible for listening to the audio during the take, as shown below.

If there are audio problems during the take, the director needs to know immediately. You can replay the footage and listen to the audio to make an on-the-spot decision about whether a reshoot needs to take place.

Your audio should be monitored by someone equipped with the microphone and a headset.

Makeup can be problematic. Outside of the acting profession, finding people who know how to apply makeup for the camera and are willing to wear it can be difficult. Try telling your 59-year-old construction worker father that he needs to wear makeup for the camera; you might find you need to recast that particular role in your movie. Your choices are then to not use makeup, which can be fine for many shoots; use actors who can use makeup and probably have their own; or ask a pro or semiprofessional to handle the makeup chores for you. A good source of the latter is a community college with a theater program, which will probably have classes in theatrical makeup and would be happy to post "makeup artists wanted" notices for you.

If you plan to use prosthetics of any kind, such as scars, wounds, or monster heads, you should either talk to the theater program people or check out a good book on making special effects makeup. There are some good tricks and suggestions for making realistic items for stage and screen, and they can be a lot of fun to make. The materials often aren't cheap, though, so see what you can do to get volunteers from the theater or movie-making community to volunteer the time and materials for your film.

Postproduction: Putting the Pieces Together

From here on out in your movie-making experience, you can follow the guidelines in the rest of this book to give your story living, breathing form. The following are some tips for your editing stint in postproduction:

Don't be afraid to toss scenes   Sometimes, despite the best efforts of planning, preparation, and production, a scene just turns out to be a clunker.

It's easier to add sound effects in post   Your story may have sound effects such as dogs barking, phones ringing, or oven timers buzzing. In most cases, it's better to add those sound effects in postproduction than trying to capture or re-create the real sound during filming. Sound effects CDs are inexpensive, have 24-bit sound on them, and are higher quality than the 16-bit audio that most camcorders capture. You also have better control over the volume, length of time, and even additional audio effects that can be applied to the sound effect.

No movie is perfect   Relax, and have fun putting the pieces together in Movie Maker. Then burn it to CD or DVD, pop it in, and show it to your friends and family. Wait for the applause and enjoy it—you've earned it!

A TOUCH **OF CLASS**

This chapter touches briefly on the wide, wonderful world of filmmaking. Hundreds of books and Web sites discuss every aspect of making movies, from camera selection to makeup, from special effects to directing, and from scheduling to film theory and history. If you have an affinity to or interest in a particular aspect of filmmaking, there are many resources available for the next time you go out to film a movie.

One resource that should be first on your list is taking a class on movie making. Community colleges and universities offer a wide selection of courses and programs, many of which are accredited. Some universities offer extension courses where the coursework is more informal and taught by hobbyists or enthusiasts such as yourself who want to share what they've learned with others.

Classes are a great way to learn more about cameras, movies, and movie making. Often the classes will divide into groups, with each group responsible for coming up with a movie idea, drafting the script, and shooting it. This gives you a way to share the work that goes into making a movie while still enjoying all the fun. Further, many of these classes have sophisticated cameras, lighting, and audio equipment that can be checked out for a weekend. As you've seen throughout this book, moviemaking can easily become a satisfying pastime.

You'll learn more in these hands-on classes than has been introduced here, and your movie making will take a leap to amazing new heights. If this book has been valuable to you and has shown you the excitement that comes from being your own filmmaker, and it encourages you to take the next step, then it has done its job. Enjoy your newfound talent and skills, and perhaps one day your hometown will see "A Film by..." on the town theater's marquee!

You can get a wealth of knowledge and experience in a filmmaking class.

Glossary

coverage
Shooting the same scene from multiple angles so that each actor's actions and reactions are captured in addition to any group shots. If two people are in a scene, coverage would include a two-shot, or a shot with both people in the frame; a shot of actor one; and a shot of actor two. This lets you cut between all three shots in editing, so you can show one actor's reactions to another actor's lines.

location
Any place in the script where action takes place. Locations can be exteriors or interiors, or even sets constructed on a soundstage.

preproduction
Everything that takes place between the decision to make a particular movie and the actual filming. This includes developing a budget, casting actors, scouting out locations, and rounding up the necessary equipment and crew.

postproduction
Everything that takes place after you have finished filming. This includes your time editing the scenes together, adding audio effects, and figuring out how to distribute your movie to friends and family.

sets
Specially constructed locations that give the illusion of being someplace else. Theaters use sets to represent other locations on stage; the same idea is used when building sets for movies.

soundstage
A special building designed for building and filming sets. These buildings give greater control over lighting, sound, and set construction than other locations such as a neighbor's garage or your mom's basement.

storyboard	A series of drawings or illustrations that show the story taking place, usually from the camera's viewpoint.
tape log	Used to record the movie name, tape number, the time code, and the scene and take number. You can print out a spreadsheet with these columns, or just keep a spiral notebook nearby for jotting down notes.
time code	A series of eight digits, represented as *nn:nn:nn:nn*, which shows hours, minutes, seconds, and frames of film shot, respectively. This allows you to edit at precise points in each clip by referring to specific time codes. Most digital video cameras insert time code onto each clip that you film.

Movie Maker 2 System Requirements

APPENDIX

If you just purchased a computer with Microsoft Windows XP on it or you installed Windows XP onto an existing computer, congratulations! You have a fantastic platform for working with digital video, audio, and special effects. Windows XP shipped with the first version of Microsoft Windows Movie Maker, a nonlinear editing studio that lets you work with video clips, images, and audio files to make your own professional-quality movies.

Understanding System Requirements

Since Windows XP went to market, Microsoft has released Movie Maker 2, an updated version of the original Movie Maker product. Before downloading and installing the new version, you should check to see if your computer meets the minimum system requirements. Although not mandatory, you'll get better performance and greater enjoyment from Movie Maker 2 if your system meets or exceeds the recommended system requirements.

MEETING THE MINIMUM SYSTEM REQUIREMENTS

You'll need the following to use Microsoft Windows Movie Maker 2:

- Microsoft Windows XP Home Edition or Windows XP Professional

- A 600 megahertz (MHz) processor, such as an Intel Pentium III, AMD Athlon, or equivalent processor

- 128 megabytes (MB) of random access memory (RAM)

- 2 gigabytes (GB) of free hard disk space

- An audio card to capture audio from external sources, such as narration for your movies

- A digital video or analog video capture card to capture video from external sources

If you already have Windows XP on your computer, you should have sufficient capabilities to start using Movie Maker 2 today. As you gain experience, you'll want to make a "wish list" to expand your computer capabilities as you go.

MEETING THE RECOMMENDED SYSTEM REQUIREMENTS

To improve your experience and the performance of Movie Maker, your system should have the following:

- A 1.5 gigahertz (GHz) processor, such as an Intel Pentium 4, an AMD Athlon XP 1500+, or equivalent processor

- 512 MB of RAM

- An Internet connection to save and send a movie to the Web or to send a movie as an attachment in an e-mail message

Upgrading Computer Components

Most people will be happy with the performance of Movie Maker on a home computer. Unlike professional editing studios, you don't need banks of expensive hardware to create a movie; off-the-shelf components work just fine.

Some people like to tinker with computers and want to find ways to optimize performance for all their applications. If you're looking for hardware-based improvements that can add zip to your editing, consider the following suggestions. They're by no means mandatory, so don't think you have to run out and purchase computer upgrades for your system.

> *Don't* attempt to install any hardware unless you first turn off and unplug your computer! You can seriously damage your computer and risk serious injury or shock yourself. Some of these upgrades require the skills, knowledge, and tools of a computer professional and shouldn't be attempted by the average user.

WARNING

CPU

If a computer is running Windows XP smoothly, then you can run Movie Maker 2 and make movies. The central processing unit (CPU) determines how fast your computer can do tasks; a 1.5 GHz processor should render a movie about two-and-a-half times faster than a 600 MHz one. A CPU upgrade will deliver immediate speed improvements to the movie-rendering process, so getting a faster CPU is a good upgrade option.

The easiest way to do this is to purchase a new computer, which will have the necessary components and configuration all set up for you. On the other hand, the cheapest way is to buy your own CPU and install it yourself. This path can be dangerous if you aren't careful; you have to understand the compatibility between CPUs and motherboards and know how to install the CPU and reconfigure key parts of the motherboard for the CPU. If you switch between processor manufacturers, such as switching from Intel to AMD, you'll need to reinstall Windows XP. Of all the upgrades, this is the one that should be done by a professional. Otherwise, you run the risk of damaging your computer, the CPU, and yourself.

If you're shopping for either a new computer or a new CPU and you're planning to render movies as a serious hobbyist or semiprofessional, consider getting a dual-CPU system. Two CPUs are definitely better than one when it comes to processor-intensive activities such as rendering, where millions of mathematical calculations are performed to generate each frame of video. Both Intel and AMD dual-processor motherboards are available, and you'll need to buy two CPU chips for the motherboard.

As with switching between processor manufacturers, if you upgrade to a dual-CPU system, you'll need to reinstall Windows XP. Windows XP requires specific internal modules to take advantage of both processors. You can't just plug in your old hard disk and fire it up—which is yet another reason you should consult a computer professional before attempting this kind of upgrade.

Finally, you've heard about CPUs generating heat. Because a CPU works hard during rendering processes, sometimes over a long period of time, the heat buildup could be problematic. Check the ventilation of your computer. Make sure the ventilation paths aren't blocked and the fans don't have extreme dust buildup. It's not often you hear about a computer failing because of excessive heat buildup, but good housekeeping will help keep it that way. And if you have a dual-CPU system, you might need to invest in additional case fans and a new power supply to handle the additional power and heat demands generated by Movie Maker.

RAM

A new take on an old saying goes, "You can never be too rich, too thin, or have too much RAM." When you make a movie, the amount of RAM your computer has will determine how big and complex the movie can be. Microsoft suggests that 512 MB of RAM for a computer running Windows XP is optimal, and many new computers today ship with that much onboard. The more RAM you have, the faster the system runs because it doesn't have to spend as much time going to the much, much slower hard disk for data.

RAM is so inexpensive and easy to install that you should put in as much RAM as your motherboard can hold. Check the motherboard details to see how much can be used effectively; some motherboards can use only 1 GB of RAM, so putting three 512 MB sticks into the motherboard wastes 512 MB.

HARD DISKS

You need about 13 GB of hard disk space for each hour of Digital Video–Audio Interleave (DV-AVI) files or movies you plan to store. Movie Maker 2 also wants about another 12 GB of temporary storage space for each hour of video you plan to render. At a minimum, you should clear off enough space from your hard disk or upgrade it so you have at least 25 GB of available space at all times.

Even better is to have two hard disks in your computer, one for your operating system and applications such as Movie Maker and the second for your movie files and rendering space. Hard disk prices are cheap, with current prices around $1 per gigabyte of storage capacity, so adding a second hard disk to your computer is a good (and inexpensive) idea in general.

When shopping for hard disks, you'll want a large hard disk with plenty of storage capacity; 80 GB should be the minimum size to start with. You should also look for hard disks with high revolutions per minute (RPM) speeds. Don't settle for one with 5,400 RPM. Your goal should be one with 7,200 RPM or higher.

Not only is hard disk speed important for overall file access times, but it's also important when capturing and exporting movie files to your camcorder. When you're capturing or exporting video files in real time, the flow of data has to keep up with the computer and camera equipment. The data will continue to flow, but if a hard disk can't keep up with the transfer, then you'll end up with dropped frames, lost color, or other quality issues.

Thus, the basic speed of the hard disk is critical for good movie quality. For these reasons, you should skip over any external Universal Serial Bus (USB) 1 hard disks or Zip drives as storage devices because the throughput is just too slow and will introduce too many errors into your movies.

The file format on your hard disks is also important, both for file handling and security reasons. If your hard disks are FAT32, you should convert them to NTFS. This allows you to work with security permissions and to work with files larger than 4 GB. To convert your file format, consult the Windows XP help file.

If you're going for a truly high-end system, you should consider installing a Redundant Array of Inexpensive Disks (RAID) controller and multiple hard disks. High-end workstations and network servers often use RAID for fault tolerance, expandability, and performance reasons. A discussion of the various types of RAID controllers and drives is far beyond the scope of this appendix, so if you need really huge amounts of hard disk space and the other benefits mentioned, talk with a computer professional about the pros and cons of installing RAID on your computer.

VIDEO CAPTURE REQUIREMENTS

You need a way to get your videos into your computer. This requires different video capture hardware depending on the source of your video.

If you have a digital video (DV) camera, you'll need either an IEEE 1394 card (also called Apple FireWire or Sony i.LINK) or an analog video capture card. IEEE 1394 is recommended for the best quality results. Many new computers come with an IEEE 1394 card already installed. If not, a number of manufacturers make a card that'll work with your computer. If you have an analog video camera or a VCR, you'll need to have an analog video capture card.

GRAPHICS CARDS

There are no specified minimum requirements for a graphics or video card. The video and movie rendering processes are less demanding of your computer's graphics card than computer-based action-packed games.

The real-time video processes you'll use for movies include capturing, previewing in Movie Maker, exporting to a camcorder, and playing a saved movie. Of these, exporting a movie to a camcorder will be the most demanding on your computer. The next most demanding is playing a saved movie in Microsoft Windows Media Player. If you don't experience smooth playback, try playing it at a lower size. If you have issues with smooth playback, it's because of factors other than your video card.

CD AND DVD BURNERS

There are no special minimum requirements for CD and DVD burners. If you have any issues when trying to use your CD burner with Movie Maker 2, first check that the burning feature of the drive is turned on. Right-click My Computer and select Explore. Next, select the drive, and right-click it. Click Properties, select the Recording tab, and then check the Enable CD Recording On This Drive option. See Figure App-1 for an example of what the page looks like. You can best handle issues with CD and DVD burning by going to online Web sites, newsgroups, and forums. The issues are different for each brand and model, and the methods of resolving them change with time.

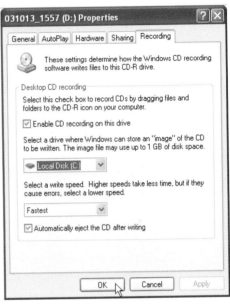

Figure App-1 The Recording tab lets you turn on the ability to burn data to your CD or DVD drive.

SOUND CARD/MICROPHONE

The minimum requirement for an audio capture device is a microphone connected to a sound card. Desktops often have microphones plugged into the sound card. Laptops often have microphones built into them, which are not easily noticeable.

Downloading and Installing Movie Maker 2

Your computer is up to speed, and you're now ready to install Movie Maker 2. If it wasn't included on your new computer, then the only way to get it is by downloading it for free from Microsoft. The installation package is about 13 MB in file size, a fairly easy download if you have a broadband connection. With a dial-up modem connection, it might take awhile.

DOWNLOADING MOVIE MAKER 2

It's best to download it as a package and then open it from your hard disk to do the actual installation. Then, if for some reason you need to reinstall Movie Maker 2, you'll have the installation package.

Download the installation package using these easy steps:

1. Connect to the Internet.

2. Click Start | All Programs | Accessories | Entertainment | Windows Movie Maker.

3. Click Help | Windows Movie Maker On The Web. You can also use Internet Explorer to go to the Movie Maker Web site at *http://www.microsoft.com/windowsxp/moviemaker/default.asp*.

4. Look for a link on the Web site to download Windows Movie Maker 2.

5. Click the link, and choose the option for saving the installation file to your hard disk.

When the download finishes, close Movie Maker before running the installation. It's best not to have a potential interference between a running application and the installation process.

INSTALLING MOVIE MAKER 2

When you're ready to do the actual installation, follow these steps:

1. Double-click the Movie Maker 2 file you downloaded.

2. Click Next on the first page of the Setup Wizard, which looks like the page in Figure App-2.

3. Click I Accept The Terms In The Licence Agreement, and then click Next.

4. Click Install. The files will install on your computer.

5. Click Finish on the last page of the Setup Wizard.

By default, the new application files will be installed into the same location as the version 1 software at C:\Program Files\Movie Maker. You can install or reinstall Movie Maker 2 at any time over a previous installation of either Movie Maker 1 or Movie Maker 2. However, once you upgrade, you can't uninstall Movie Maker 2 and return to the previous version unless you use System Restore. See the next section for more information about System Restore.

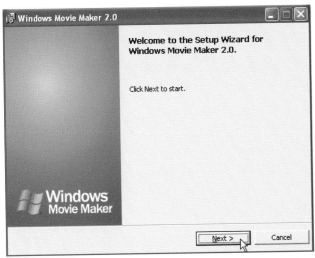

Figure App-2 The Setup Wizard walks you through the short steps to install Movie Maker 2.

Troubleshooting Tips and Suggestions

The following sections offer some troubleshooting tips in case something goes wrong when using Movie Maker.

USING SYSTEM RESTORE

Windows XP includes System Restore, which lets you go backward in time to help resolve what might be a significant computer issue. If you expect to be adding hardware devices to capture video, update your video driver, or do any other computer enhancements while you get into video editing, you might run into an unexpected issue. System Restore lets you undo the changes you made and return your system to its previous state. It's also a good way to take a snapshot of your operating system and applications, install trial versions of software, work with the trial versions, and then restore your system as if the software had never been installed. Windows XP takes these snapshots automatically for you, or you can manually take a snapshot just before installing new software.

It's a good idea to have System Restore running in the background. To verify that System Restore is on, click Start | All Programs | Accessories | System Tools | System Restore. If it's running you should see a Welcome To System Restore page, as shown in Figure App-3. If it's off, you'll get a small dialog box saying "System Restore has been turned off. Do you want to turn on System Restore now?" Click Yes to turn on System Restore.

If you need to restore an older snapshot, open System Restore using the previous steps. Click Restore My Computer To An Earlier Time, and then click Next. A calendar appears, with restore points listed in bold, as shown in Figure App-4. If more than one restore point was created on that day, they'll appear on the right. Select one, and then click Next. A warning page appears, asking you to confirm the restore. Read it carefully, and click Cancel if you don't want to continue. Otherwise, click Next. Your computer will revert to the older save point after restarting.

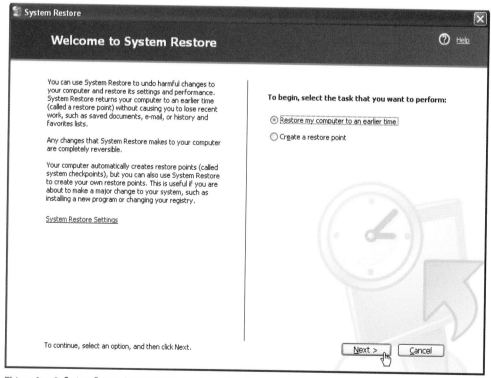

Figure App-3 System Restore lets you go back to the point before you installed an application.

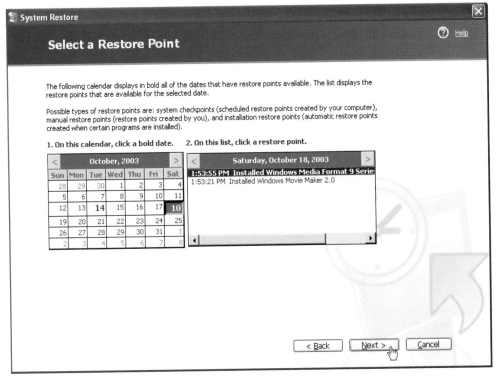

Figure App-4 The calendar shows you when the last restore points were created.

TROUBLESHOOTING PERFORMANCE ISSUES

Video processes can use your computer's CPU and hard disk to such a high degree that the process can be susceptible to "hiccups" when interrupted by other tasks or processes. The most critical time is when you export a finished movie to a camcorder. The next most critical time is when you capture your video files from your camcorder or other device. The rendering process, when your computer is saving your new movie, is much less critical than during capture or export. A quick way to see what is running is to right-click an empty space on the taskbar and select Task Manager.

The first tab will show you the applications currently running, and the second tab will show you the processes. If you like graphs, check the third tab of the Task Manager to see how busy your computer's CPU is and how much it needs to go to the hard disk page file; Figure App-5 shows you the Task Manager graphic display. If you encounter problems when exporting or capturing files, close all applications except Movie Maker, and close or stop as many services and applets that are running in the system notification area (the far-right side of the taskbar). Check the Task Manager again to see if the CPU usage has dropped, and then try exporting or capturing your files again.

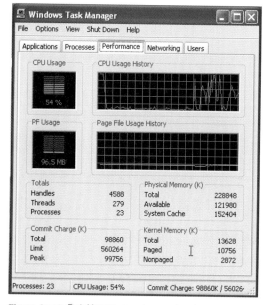

Figure App-5 Task Manager can show you how busy your computer is when working on your tasks.

Movie Maker performance is also affected by disk fragmentation. Fragmentation occurs when files are saved in pieces on your hard disk. When there are many file fragments, your computer slows down because it takes longer to work with file fragments than with large contiguous files.

Disk defragmentation reorders the file fragments so each file is in one place, not fragmented. It's an important tune-up process for your movie files that also frees up more empty space on your hard disk. This is especially important for a critical video operation such as saving a movie on a camcorder tape. You don't want the computer to have to slow down to look for the next part of a movie file because it's busy sending it over your FireWire connection to the camcorder. The hard disk condition is most important during that process.

To defragment your hard disk, follow these steps:

1. Click Start | All Programs | Accessories | System Tools | Disk Defragmenter.

2. Select a drive letter, and then click Analyze.

3. If Disk Defragmenter recommends you defragment the drive, click Defragment.

This process can take quite awhile depending on the degree of fragmentation, so go grab a beverage and wait for the defragmenter to finish. Figure App-6 shows a drive being defragmented. You can defragment all your drive letters and hard disks this way, especially the ones where you store your movie files and where the Movie Maker temporary storage area is kept.

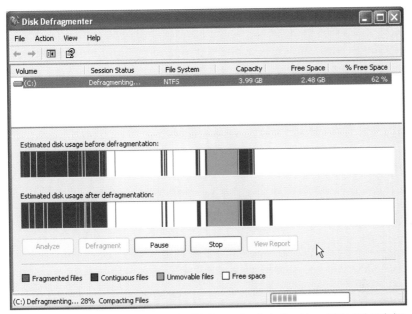

Figure App-6 Defragmenting your hard disk will help speed up tasks like video capture and rendering.

If the amount of free space is still limited after you run Disk Defragmenter, try removing temporary or unneeded files from your hard disk. The biggest culprits here are temporary files from surfing the Internet, which tend to hang around long after a Web page is useful. Another Windows XP utility, Disk Cleanup, takes care of that task for you. Click Start | All Programs | Accessories | System Tools | Disk Cleanup. Select a drive you want to clean, and click OK. It'll scan your drive and list the amount of free space you can reclaim from your hard disk. Click the boxes so a check appears in each item you want cleaned, and then click OK. Windows XP will clean up the unneeded files for you.

DEALING WITH MPEG IMPORT ISSUES

Sometimes MPEG files can be misleading. A video MPEG-1 file will import without any problems into Movie Maker, but an MPEG-2 file won't. MPEG-2 files and issues with them are fairly common. Playing back and importing MPEG-2 content completely depends on the MPEG-2 decoder installed on the particular hardware device.

MPEG-2 files are highly compressed and don't make good source files for video editing and movie making. They're meant to be viewed and not edited, unless you're using some specialty hardware or software that you received with your hardware that makes the MPEG-2 files.

One of the problems is trying to import MPEG-2 files from micro-camcorders. The camcorders store and output a highly compressed MPEG-2 file that Movie Maker usually can't import. To work around this and still use the file, you'll need to use the software that came with your camcorder to do the capturing and then use other software to convert it into a format you can import into Movie Maker 2.

If you need to convert a video file such as one from a micro-camcorder, you should think about a couple of factors. What quality is the video file you're starting with? What are you planning to do with the clips from it? If you're starting with highly compressed MPEG-2 files and expecting to make high-quality DVDs for your Movie Maker project, you might have to rethink your options. It's much better to assess the movie quality up front rather than putting hundreds of hours into editing sessions and then finding you can't make high-quality DVDs from the material. Invest in a quick 15-second sample conversion, editing, and burning. If you're happy with the final output, then invest whatever hours you need for the full production.

CONVERTING MACINTOSH MOVIES TO MOVIE MAKER FORMAT

One of the video file types you'll often come across is Apple QuickTime. It's used on most Apple computers and sometimes on Windows-based computers. The files have an MOV file extension and need a special QuickTime viewer to play on Windows XP. These files have the versatility of being viewable on both Windows and on Apple computers. But you can't play them in the Windows Media Player or import them into Movie Maker 2.

How do you watch movies from Movie Maker 2 on a Macintosh, and how do you use movies from Apple iMovie in Movie Maker?

To import a QuickTime MOV file, convert it first to an AVI file using a utility such as Rad Video Tools, a free download from *http://www.radgametools.com/bnkdown.htm*, shown in Figure App-7. Then import the AVI file into Movie Maker 2, and you should be able to use the footage and audio as usual.

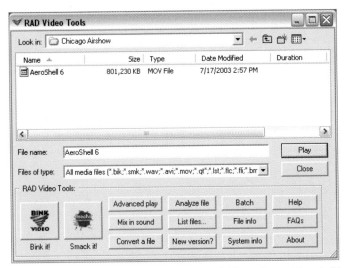

Figure App-7 The RAD Video Tools lets you import MOV files and convert them to AVI.

For other file conversion questions or problems with specific files, check the book's Web site at *http://www.papajohn.org*. Developments in these areas are dynamic, and this Web site provides the most up-to-date information about making, viewing, and converting video files so you can play or use them in video editing on another platform.

Index

About the Authors

John "PapaJohn" Buechler is a Microsoft Most Valuable Professional (MVP) recognized for his contributions to the community of Windows Movie Maker users. You'll get to know him well as you read this book and use the supporting newsgroups and forums. His Movie Maker Web site with the book's online companion is constantly evolving, and you'll find him to be a friend in addition to a teacher.

Wherever Movie Maker is, he is. His home is in Kalamazoo; he and his wife Bernadette visit their children and grandchildren often, taking pictures and video for the next productions.

Michael S. Toot is a Seattle-based writer and consultant who writes books on desktop applications and server-side middleware. He has been employed in the computer industry since 1992; prior to that he was a litigation attorney in the state of Washington. When not writing books, he can be found renovating his 95-year-old home with his wife and two cats, sailing on Puget Sound, or reading.

Get a **Free**
e-mail newsletter, updates,
special offers, links to related books,
and more when you

register online!

Register your Microsoft Press® title on our Web site and you'll get a FREE subscription to our e-mail newsletter, *Microsoft Press Book Connections.* You'll find out about newly released and upcoming books and learning tools, online events, software downloads, special offers and coupons for Microsoft Press customers, and information about major Microsoft® product releases. You can also read useful additional information about all the titles we publish, such as detailed book descriptions, tables of contents and indexes, sample chapters, links to related books and book series, author biographies, and reviews by other customers.

Registration is easy. Just visit this Web page and fill in your information:
http://www.microsoft.com/mspress/register

Microsoft
